Teachi

Teaching Yourself
HINDI

DR. KRISHNA NAND VERMA

MAHAVEE**R**
PUBLISHERS

Published by
MAHAVEER PUBLISHERS
4764/2A, 23-Ansari Road, Daryaganj
New Delhi - 110002
Ph. : 011 – 66629669–79–89
Fax : 011 – 41563419
e-mail : mahaveerpublishers@gmail.com

First Edition : 2003
Second Revised Edition : 2005
Revised Edition : 2011

Teaching Yourself Hindi
ISBN : 9788190219600

Distributed by
VAIBHAV BOOK SERVICE
e-mail : vaibhavbookservice@gmail.com

Printed by Jaico Printers, New Delhi

Preface

Hindi is one of the oldest languages of the world. National language of India, it is spoken in over 120 countries – wherever there is an Indian, Hindi is there! In its content, structure and make-up, writing and speaking, the language is simple, scientific and logical. Easy to understand, it is a wonderful language.

Also, it is a key to reach the greatest 'culture centre' and the 'biggest market' – India – of the world. But being different from the languages of Europe, Africa and some other parts of the world it might seem difficult to learn. But, in fact, it is not that – and especially so when one has the right tool to learn it.

And this small book is, let me put it with all humility, that 'right tool'. It will help the learner to have a working knowledge of the great language in a very brief time and that, too, without doing anything like burning the midnight oil or exhausting oneself too much. Just 30 minutes to one hour or so each day is what this book will like to keep oneself with for some time to win the battle – to be able to communicate in Hindi – adequately, fluently.

The book has been designed in such a way that the learner doesn't lose interest, speed and comprehension of the language at any point. Each chapter covers a part of life spent each day at different places, in different situations. Nothing irrelevant or boring has been allowed to come in.

It is the simplest way to learn Hindi.

Author

Preface

Contents

Contents

The alphabet & pronunciation

The script of Hindi language is known as *Devanagri*. It consists of 12 vowels and 36 consonants. To obtain a working knowledge of the vowels, the reader is advised to view the following chart.

	Vowels	English equivalent	Phonetic symbol	Guide to pronunciation
1.	अ	A	A'	As 'u' in cut.
2.	आ	AA	Ā	As 'a' in what
3.	इ	I	I	As 'i' in bit.
4.	ई	EE	EE	As 'ea' in beat.
5.	उ	U	U	As 'u' in put.
6.	ऊ	oo	oo	As 'oo' in hoot.
7.	ए	E	E'	As 'a' in rate.
8.	ऐ	AI	AI	As 'a' in rack.

9. ओ	*o*	*o*	As 'oa' in goat.
10. औ	*AU*	*AU*	As 'o' in floppy.
11. अं	*AN*	*AN′*	As 'un in clung.
12. अः	*AH*	*AH′*	As 'ah' in blah.

The consonants have a basic difference from Roman alphabets. A Roman alphabet is a HALF LETTER in itself until a vowel is placed following it.

For example : 1. 'W' has no phonetic existence of its own unless it is written as WATER or WILD where it becomes *'Wā'* or *'Wai'*.

2. 'C' has no phonetic existence of its own unless it is written as CATCH or CONFIRM where it sounds as *'Cai'* or *'cun'*.

On the other hand, in Hindi, every consonant is complete within itself because it has the vowel 'a' inherently incorporated in it. It has a phonetic sound of its own. Any additional vowel only changes its phonetics accordingly.

For example : 1. The first consonant 'क' (*Ka*) is spoken as *Ka'* if written as such. By adding vowels further, it may of course be turned into की (*KEE*) or के (*KE'*).

2. The twenty first consonant 'प' (PA) is 'independently spoken as PA'. An additional vowel may change its phonetics as पी (PEE) or पु (PU) accordingly.

The reader may note that to make 'क' (*KA*) sound like *'K'*, the inherent vowel 'a' has to be separated from 'क' or any other consonant. And now क is written with an oblique stroke under it which is known as *'hãlãnt'*. क् is exact equivalent of K. Similarly प्, म्, ग्, are exact equivalents of P, M, G. respectively. These have no sound of their own.

Now look at following chart of 36 consonants :

Consonant	English equivalent	Phonetic symbol	Guide to pronunciation
1. क	KA	KA´	As 'cu' in cut.
2. ख	KHA	KHA´	Khakez times
3. ग	GA	GA´	As 'gi' in girl.
4. घ	GHA	GHA´	As Gha in Ghana
5. ङ	ANGAH	NG	As 'ung' in clung.
6. च	CHA	CHA´	As 'chu' in church.
7. छ	CHHA	CHHA´	NIL
8. ज	JA	JA´	As 'ju' in jug.
9. झ	JHA	JHA´	NIL
10. ञ	YAN	YA´N´	NIL
11. ट	TA (hard)	ṬA´	As 'tu' in turtle.
12. ठ	THA (hard)	ṬHA´	As 'Tha' in Lothar (German literatteur)
13. ड	DA (hard)	ḌA´	As 'du' in dump.
14. ढ	DHA (hard)	ḌHA´	As 'Dha' in Dhaka
15. ण	NA (hard)	ṆA´	NIL

[Denoted by an underscribed 'h']

16. त	TA	TA´ (Soft)	As the last 't' pronounced in Tashkent./ As 't' is spoken in Russian, French etc.
17. थ	THA	THA´ (Soft)	As 'tha' in Pythagorus.
18. द	DA	DA´ (Soft)	As the Pronounced as such.
19. ध	DHA	DHA´ (Soft)	NIL
20. न	NA	NA´ (Soft)	As 'nu' in nursing.
21. प	PA	PA´	As 'pu' in puckered.
22. फ	PHA	PHA´	As 'fu' in fur.
23. ब	BA	BA´	As 'bu' in bubble.
24. भ	BHA	BHA´	NIL
25. म	MA	MA´	As 'mu' in mutter.
26. य	YA	YA´	As 'yu' in yuppie.
27. र	RA	RA´	As 'ru' in rub.
28. ल	LA	LA´	As 'Lo' in Love.
29. व	WA/VA	WA´/VA´	As 'wo' in word.

30.	श	*SHA*	*SHA´*	As 'shu' in shut.
31.	ष	*SHA*	*SHA´*	NIL
32.	स	*SA*	*SA´*	As 'si' in sir.
33.	ह	*HA*	*HA´*	As 'hu' in hurt.
34.	क्ष	*KSHA*	*KSHA´*	NIL
35.	त्र	*ṬRA*	*TRA´* (soft)	NIL
36.	ज्ञ	*JNA*	*GYAN´*	NIL

The reader is advised to keep in mind the phonetic symbol of each alphabet.

After going through the whole List of Hindi vowels and consonants, the next step that is important in understanding Hindi pronunciation, is, how to JOIN a consonant with a vowel.

Here we take the consonant 'क' (KA´) and see how all the 12 vowels can be joinned with it respectively to produce 12 different forms of 'क' (KA') :

1. क्+अ   = क   As 'cu' in cut.
   (K+A   = KA´)
2. क्+आ   = का   As 'ka' in kamikaze.
   (K+AA   = KĀ)

3. क्+इ   = कि   As 'ki' in kiss.
   (K+I   = KI)

4. क्+ई   = की   As 'kee' in keen.
   (K+EE   = KEE)

5. क्+उ   = कु   As 'cu' in cuckoo.
   (K+U   = KU)

6. क्+अ   = कू   As 'coo' in cook.
   (K+OO   = KOO)

7. क्+ए   = के   As 'Ka' in Kate.
   (K+E   = KE')

8. क्+ऐ   = कै   As 'Ca' in California.
   (K+AI   = KAI)

9. क्+ओ   = को   As 'coa' in coarse.
   (K+O   = KO')

10. क्+औ   = कौ   As 'co' in copy.
    (K+AU   = KAU)

11. क्+अं   = कं   As 'kan' in kangaroo.
    (K+AN´ = KAN´)

12. क्+अः   = कः
    (K+A´H = KA´H)

Now it may be satisfactorily assumed that the
reader has been, by now, well acquainted with all

the alphabets, their respective pronunciation and how a vowel is joinned with a consonant.

The next step, naturally, should be 'formation of a Hindi sentence.'

Formation of a Hindi Sentence

A few basic differences between structures of Hindi and English sentences are following.

1. In English the VERB is placed immediately after the subject and the object, if present, comes after the verb.

   But in Hindi, the verb is usually situated at the distal end of the sentence and the rest every other word has its place in between the subject at one end and the verb on the other.

   Example: a. Jacob went to the hospital.

   Jacob aspátāl gáyā.

   (जेकब अस्पताल गया)

   b. Rajani is eating biscuts.

   Rajani biskit khā ráhee hai.

   (रजनी बिस्किट खा रही है।)

c. A beautiful girl is running.

*E´k sundár Ládki dauḍ
ráhee hai*

(एक सुन्दर लड़की दौड़ रही है।)

Note : This THIRD sentence has no
object or adverb, so in this case
the sentences in both the language appear almost same
regarding the place of verb. But
it must be noted that, even here,
the AUXILIARY VERB 'is' is
placed BEFORE the main verb
while its Hindi substitue 'है' is
placed AFTER the main verb.

2. As in English language, the verb in a Hindi
sentence undergoes a number of changes
according to the SUBJECT and TENSE.

What our reader is required to note
is that - in Hindi, the verb has to change
according to TWO more factors:

● The NUMBER and the GENDER of
the OBJECT - in case of a TRAN-
SITIVE verb.

● The NUMBER and the GENDER of
the SUBJECT - in case of an INTRAN-
SITIVE verb.

A further illustration would be quite useful.

a.   **A transitive verb : Eat = khana = खाना**

Subject = Devashish (a male)

Object = I. Mango (male)

II. Bread (female)

Tense   = Past indiefinite.

1. Devashish ate A MANGO.

    Devashish ne' ék ām KHAYA.

2. Devashish ate A BREAD

    Devashish ne' ék rotee KHAYEE.

3. Devashish ate TWO MANGOES.

    Devashish ne' do ām KHAYE'.

4. Devashish ate FOUR BREADS.

    *Devashish   ne'   chār   rotiyān
KHĀYEEN'.*

Here, depending upon the number and the gender of the object, we find that FOUR forms of vereb
have been used. They, being TRANSITIVE, solely

depend upon the object. Any change in subject pro-
duces no change in the verb.

    b. **An intransitive verb** : sleép = soná‿= सोना

Subject   =   I. Devashish (male/singular)

                  II. Sangeeta (female/singular)

                  III. Boys (male/plural)

                  IV. Girls (female/plural)

Tense   =   Present indefinite.

1.   Devashish sleeps.

     Devashish SOTĀ HAI.

2.   Sangeeta sleeps.

     Sangeeta SOTEE HAI.

3.   The boys sleep.

     Ladke' SOTE´ HAIN.

4.   The girls sleep

     Láḍkiyān SOTEE Hain.

So these are a few examles trying to emphasize how Hindi differs from English. The reader is
advised to use his/her INSTINCT also along with
the INTELLECT to have a broader grasp of this
oriental language.

At the end of this chapter, a set of about 22 sentences has been provided.

The reader may not find any particular order in those sentences, our effort in doing so has been just to provide the reader with a READY MADE STOCK of all possible sentences which he/she is most likely to need. We hope, it helps.

PROTOTYPE   SENTENCES

A. Verb = Go = Jana = जाना

I. Subject = FIRST PERSON, SINGULAR NUMBER

1. I go = *Main jātā hoon* = मैं जाता हूं (m)
   [f = jatee hoon]

2. I am going = *Main jā ráhā hoon* = मैं जा रहा हूं (m) [f = rahee hoon]

3. I have gone = *Main jā chukā hoon* = मैं जा चुका हूं (m) [f = chukee hoon]

4. I have been going = *Main jātā ráhā hoon* = मैं जाता रहा हूं (m) [f = jatee rahee hoon]

5. I went = *Main gáyā* = मैं गया (m) [f = gayee]

6. I was going = *Main jā ráhā thā* = मैं जा रहा था (m) [f = rahee thee]

7. I had gone = *Main jā chukā thā* = मैं जा चुका था (m)
   [f = chukee thee]

8. I had been going = *Main jātā ráhā thā* = मैं जाता
   रहा था (m) [f = jatee rahee thee]

9. I will go = *Main jā-ungā* = मैं जाउंगा (m)
   [f = ja-ungee]

10. I will be going = *Main jā ráhā ho-ungā* = मैं जा
    रहा होऊंगा (m) [f = rahee ho-ungee]

11. I will have gone = *Main jā chukā ho-ungā* = मैं जा
    चुका होउंगा (m) [f = chukee ho-ungee]

12. I will have going = *Main jātā ráhā ho-unga* = मैं
    जाता रहा होउंगा = [f = jatee rahee ho-ungee]

13. I can go = *Main jā sákátā hoon* = मैं जा सकता
    हूं (m) [f = sakatee hoon]

14. I could go = *Main jā sákátā thā* = मैं जा सकता
    था (m) [f = sakatee thee]

15. I will be able to go = *Main jā sákoongā* = मैं जा
    सकूंगा (m) [f = sakoongee]

16. Can I go? = *Kya main jā sákátā hoon?* = क्या
    मैं जा सकता हूं? (m) [f = sakatee hoon]

17. Could I go? = *Kya main jā sákátā thā?* = क्या
    मैं जा सकता था? (m) [f = sakatee thee.]

18. Will I be able to go? = *Kyā main jā sakoongā?* =
    क्या मैं जा सकूंगा. (m) [f = saoogee]

19. I want to go = *Main Jānā chāhátā hoon'* = मैं जाना

चाहता हूँ (m) [f = chahatee hoon]

20. I wanted to go = *Main Jānā chāhátā thā* = मैं
    जाना चाहता था (m) [f = chahatee thee]

21. I would like to go = *Main jānā chahoongā* =
    मैं जाना चाहूँगा (m) [f = chahoongee]

● To make a NEGATIVE sentence, NAHEEN has
  to be added immediately after the subject 'MAIN' :

  Eg. *Main náheen jātā hoon* = I do not go.

  Main náheen gáyā   = I did not go.

  Naheen, main náheen

  jā ungā   = No, I will not go.

● To emphasize the AFFIRMATION, *hán* = हाँ
  has to be added right in the beginning which
  is same as 'yes' :

  Eg : 1. Yes, I had gone = *Hán, main jā chukā thā*

  2. Yes, I will go   = *Han, main jā-ungā*.

22. I should go/ I must go/ I ought to go = *Mujhe
    jānā chahiye* = मुझे जाना चाहिए (m/f).

II. Subject : FIRST PERSON, PLURAL, Male or female

Hindi equivalent for WE is *hám* = हम. How
the form of verb changes, when the subject changes
from 'I' to 'we', has been shown in following sentences. The sequence of the sentences is same as
in previous section :

1. We go = *Hám játé hain* = हम जाते हैं. (m/f)

2. We are going = *Hám já ráhé hain* = हम जा रहे हैं. (m/f)

3. ———— *Já chuké hain* = जा चुके हैं. (m/f)

4. ———— *Játé ráhé hain* = जाते रहे हैं. (m/f)

5. ———— *gáyé* = ———— गये (m/f)

6. ———— *jā ráhé thé* = ————जा रहे थे. (m/f)

7. ———— *Já chuké thé* = ————जा चुके थे. (m/f)

8. ———— *Játé ráhé thé* = ————जा रहे थे. (m/f)

9. ———— *jāyéngé* = ———— जायेंगे. (m/f)

10. ———— *Já ráhé hongé* = ———— जा रहे होंगे. (m/f)

11. ———— *Já chuké hongé* = ———— जा चुके होंगे. (m/f)

12. ———— *Játé ráhé hongé* = ———— जाते रहे होंगे. (m/f)

13. ———— *Já sákáté hain* = ———— जा सकते हैं. (m/f)

14. ———— *Já sákáté thé* = ———— जा सकते थे. (m/f)

15. ------------ Jā sákéngé = ------------ जा सकेंगे. (m/f)

16. ------------ Kyā hám jā sákáté hain? = क्या हम जा सकते हैं? (m/f)

17. ------------ Kya hám jā sákáté thé? = क्या हम जा सकते थे? (m/f)

18. ------------ Kyā hám jā sākéngé? = क्या हम जा सकेंगे? (m/f)

19. ------------ Hám jānā chāhté hain = हम जाना चाहते हैं (m/f)

20. ------------ Hám jānā chāhté thé = हम जाना चाहते थे. (m/f)

21. ------------ Hám jānā chāhéngé = हम जाना चाहेंगे. (m/f)

22. ------------ Hámein jānā chāhiyé = हमें जाना चाहिए. (m/f)

III. Subject : SECOND PERSON

Hindi equivalent for YOU is tum = तुम. It may be 'masculine' as well as 'feminine' and the form of verb changes accordingly. The Sequence of the sentences is same as in previous section :

1. You go = *Tum játé ho*   =   तुम जाते हो. (m)

         játee ho = ...जाती हो. (f)

2. You are going = *Tum já ráhé ho* = तुम जा रहे हो. (m)

         ....*jā ráhee ho* = ... जा रही हो. (f)

3. You have gone = *Tum já chuké ho* = तुम जा चुके हो. (m)

         ....*chukee ho* = ... चुकी हो. (f)

4. .... = *Tum játé ráhé ho* = तुम जा रहे हो. (m)

         ....*játee ráhee ho* = ... जाती रही हो. (f)

5. You went = *Tum gáyé* = तुम गये. (m)

         ....*gáyee* = ... गयी. (f)

6. .... = ...*jā rāhé thé* = ... जा रहे थे. (m)
........*jā rāhee thee* = ...जा रही थी (f)

7. .... = ...*jā chuké thé* = ...जा चुके थे (m)
........*jā chukee thee* = ...जा चुकी थी (f)

8. .... = ...*jāté rāhé thé* = ...जाते रहे थे (m)
........*jātee rahee thee* = ...जाती रही थी (f)

9. You will go = *Tum jāogé* = तुम जाओगे. (m)
........*jāogee* = ...जाओगी. (f)

10. .... = ...*jā rāhé hogé* = ...जा रहे होगे. (m)
........*jā rāhee hogee* = ...जा रही होगी. (f)

11. .... = ...*jā chuké hogé* = ...जा चुके होगे. (m)
........*jā chukee hogee* = ...जा चुकी होगी. (f)

12. .... = ...*jāté rahé hogé* = ...जाते रहे होगे (m)
........*jātee rahee hogee* = ...जाती रही होगी (f)

13. ...... = ...jā sákáte ho = ...जा सकते हो. (m)

    ......jā sákátee ho = ...जा सकती हो. (f)

14. ...... = ...jā sákáte thé = ...जा सकते थे. (m)

    ......jā sákátee thee = ...जा सकती थी. (f)

15. ...... = ...jā sákogé = ...जा सकोगे (m)

    ......jā sákogee = ...जा सकोगी (f)

16. ...... = Kyā tum jā sákáte ho? = क्या तुम जा सकते हो? (m)

    Kyā tum jā sákátee ho? = क्या तुम जा सकती हो (f)

17. ...... = Kyā tum jā sákaté thé? = क्या तुम जा सकते थे? (m)

    Kyā tum jā sákátee thee? = क्या तुम जा सकती थी (f)

18. ...... = Kyā tum jā sákogé? = क्या तुम जा सकोगे? (m)

    Kyā tum jā sákogee? = क्या तुम जा सकोगी? (f)

19. ...... = Tum jānā chāhāté ho = तुम जाना चाहते हो? (m)

    Tum jānā chāhátee ho = तुम जाना चाहती हो (f)

20. .... = *Tum jānā chāhāté the* = तुम जाना चाहते थे (m)

 Tum jānā chāhātee thee = तुम जाना चाहती थी (f)

21. .... = *Tum jānā chāhogé* = तुम जाना चाहोगे. (m)

 Tum jānā chāhogee = तुम जाना चाहोगी (f)

22. .... = *Tumhéń jānā chāhiyé* = तुम्हें जाना चाहिए. (m)

 Tumhéń jānā chāhiyé = तुम्हें जाना चाहिए (f)

IV. Subject : THIRD PERSON, SINGULAR NUMBER

This section, dealing with third person and singular number, differs only slightly from the previous one.

1. He goes = *Wáh jātā hai* = वह जाता है (m)

 She goes = *Wáh jātee hai* = वह जाती है (f)

2. .... = ...*jā ráhā hai* = ...जा रहा है. (m)

 .... = ...*jā ráhee hai* = ...जा रही है. (f)

3. .... = jā chukā hai = ...जा चुका है (m)
.... = jā chukee hai = ...जा चुकी है (f)

4. .... = jātā rāhā hai = ...जाता रहा है (m)
.... = jātee rāhee hai = ...जाती रही है (f)

5. He went = Wáh gáyā = वह गया (m)
   She went = Wáh gayee = वह गयी (f)

6. .... = jā rāhā thā = ...जा रहा था. (m)
.... = jā rāhee thee = ...जा रही थी. (f)

7. .... = jā chukā thā = ...जा चुका था (m)
.... = jā chukee thee = ...जा चुकी थी (f)

8. .... = jātā rāhā thā = ...जाता रहा था. (m)
.... = jātee rāhee thee = ...जाती रही थी (f)

9.	He will go	= *Wáh jāyégā*	= वह जाएगा. (m)
	She will go	= *Wáh jāyégee*	= वह जाएगी (f)
10.	....	= ....*jā rāhā hogā*	= ....जा रहा होगा. (m)
		= ....*jā ráhee hogee*	= ....जा रही होगी (f)
11.	....	= ....*jā chukā hogā*	= ....जा चुका होगा (m)
		= ....*jā chukee hogee*	= ....जा चुकी होगी (f)
12.	....	= ....*jātā rāhā hogā*	= ....जाता रहा होगा. (m)
		= ....*jātee ráhee hogee*	= ....जाती रही होगी (f)
13.	....	= ....*jā sákátā hai*	= ....जा सकता है (m)
		= ....*jā sákátee hai*	= ....जा सकती है (f)
14.	....	= ....*jā sákátā thā*	= ....जा सकता था. (m)
		= ....*jā sákátee thee*	= ....जा सकती थी (f)

15.	....	=	.............jā sákégā	=	.........जा सकेंगा. (m)
	....	=	.............jā sákégee	=	.........जा सकेंगी (f)
16.	....	=	Kyā wáh jā sákátā hai?	=	क्या वह जा सकता है? (m)
			Kyā wáh jā sakatee hai?	=	क्या वह जा सकती है? (f)
17.	....	=	Kyā wáh jā sakatā tha?	=	क्या वह जा सकता था? (m)
			Kyā wáh jā sákátee thee?	=	क्या वह जा सकती थी? (f)
18.	....	=	Kyā wáh jā sákégā?	=	क्या वह जा सकेगा? (m)
			Kyā wáh jā sákégee?	=	क्या वह जा सकेगी? (f)
19.	....	=	Wáh jānā chāhātā hai	=	वह जाना चाहता है (m)
			Wah jānā chāhātee hai	=	वह जाना चाहती है (f)
20.	....	=	Wah jānā chāhātā thā	=	वह जाना चाहता था (m)
			Wah jānā chāhātee thee	=	वह जाना चाहती थी (f)
21.	....	=	Wah jānā chāhégā	=	वह जाना चाहेगा (m)
			Wah jānā chāhégee	=	वह जाना चाहेगी (f)
22.	....	=	Usko jānā chāhiyé	=	उसको जाना / चाहिए (m)
			Usko jānā chāhiye	=	उसको जाना चाहिए (f)

V. Subject : THIRD PERSON, PLURAL NUMBER

Hindi equivalent of THEY is *Wé* = वे. The following sentences are based on this particular subject but they cover the similar subjects like THESE and THOSE as well.

1. They go   = *Wé jāte hain*   = वे जाते हैं (m)
   They go   = *Wé jātee hain*   = वे जाती हैं (f)

2. They are going = *Wé jā ráhé hain* = वे जा रहे हैं (m)
   They are going = *Wé jā rāhee hain* = वे जा रही हैं (f)

3. .... = *Wé jā chuké hain* = वे जा चुके हैं (m)

   .... = *Wé jā chukee hain* = वे जा चुकी हैं (f)

4. .... = *Wé jāté ráhé hain* = वे जाते रहे हैं (m)

   .... = *Wé jātee rāhee hain* = वे जाती रही हैं (f)

5. They went   = *Wé gáyé* = वे गये (m)

           = *Wé gáyeeń* = वे गयीं (f)

6. They were going = *Wé jā ráhé thé* = वे जा रहे थे (m)

           = *Wé jā rahee theeń* = वे जा रही थीं. (f)

7. .... = *Wé jā chuké thé* = वे जा चुके थे. (m)

           = *Wé jā chukee theeń* = वे जा चुकी थीं (f)

8. .... = *Wé jāte ráhé thé* = वे जाते रहे थें (m)

           = *Wé jātee ráhee theeń* = वे जाती रही थीं (f)

9. They will go   = *Wé jāyéngé* = वे जायेंगे (m)

           = *Wé jāyéngee* = वे जायेंगी (f)

10. .... = *Wé jā ráhé hongé* = वे जा रहे होंगे (m)

           = *Wé jā ráhee hongee* = वे जा रही होंगी (f)

11. .... = Wé jā chuké hongé = वे जा चुके होंगे (m)

      !! = Wé jā chukee hongee = वे जा चुकी होंगी (f)

12. .... = Wé jāté rāhé hongé = वे जाते रहे होंगे. (m)

      = Wé jātee rāhee hongee = वे जाती रही होंगी. (f)

13. They can go = Wé jā sākáté hain = वे जा सकते हैं (m)

      = Wé jā sākátee hain = वे जा सकती हैं (f)

14. They could go = Wé jā sākáté thé = वे जा सकते थे (m)

      = Wé jā sākátee theeń = वे जा सकती थीं. (f)

15. They would be able to go. = Wé jā sākéngé = वे जा सकेंगे (m)

      = Wé jā sākéngee = वे जा सकेंगी. (f)

16. Can they go? = Kyā wé jā sākáté hain = क्या वे जा सकते हैं? (m)

      = Kyā wé jā sākátee hainń = क्या वे जा सकती हैं? (f)

17. Could they go?

= *Kyā wé jā sákáté thé* = क्या वे जा सकते थे? (m)

= *Kyā wé jā sákátee theeń* = क्या वे जा सकती थीं? (f)

18. Would they be able to go?

= *Kyā wé jā sákéngé?* = क्या वे जा सकेंगे? (m)

= *Kyā wé jā sákéngee?* = क्या वे जा सकेंगी? (f)

19. They want to go.

= *Wé jānā chāháté haiń.* = वे जाना चाहते हैं? (m)

= *Wé jānā chāhátee haiń* = वे जाना चाहती हैं? (f)

20. They wanted to go.

= *Wé jānā chāháte thé* = वे जाना चाहते थे (m)

= *Wé jānā chāhátee theeń* = वे जाना चाहती थीं (f)

21. They wuld like to go.

= *Wé jānā chāhéngé* = वे जाना चाहेंगे. (m)

= *Wé jānā chāhéngee* = वे जाना चाहेंगी (f)

22. .... = *Unko jānā chāhiyé* = उनको जाना चाहिए (m)

= *Unko jānā chāhiyé* = उनको जाना चाहिए (f)

With this last section of SPECIMEN SENTENCES, we sum up this chapter. And hope that the reader would be able to form sentences with any other verb once he/she has thoroughly grasped the patterns given in the above five sections.

A review of Hindi verbs

As in English, Hindi language has :

(a) MAIN verbs

(b) AUXILLIARY verbs

The auxilliary verbs are given systematically in the following table :

Subject :	I person Singular	I person Plural	II person	III person Singular	III person Plural
Tense :					
1. Present :	Hoon' ंहूँ	Hain' हैं	Ho हो	Hai है	Hain' हैं

	Thā/Thee	Thé	Thé	Thā/Thee	Thé/Theen'
2. Past :	था थी (m) (f)	थे (m)	थे	था थी (m) (f)	थे थीं (m) (f)
3. Future :	Gā/Gee गा गी (m) (f)	Gé गे (m)	Gé गे	Ga/Gee गा गी (m) (f)	Gé/Gee गे गी (m) (f)

While going through the chapter on formation of sentences, the reader will gradually become familiar with the use of above auxilliary words.

Regarding MAIN VERBS, they are of two types. One type consists of, as in English, a SINGLE WORD and in first form, all end with nā (ना) :

सोना	=	sonā	=	to sleep
जाना	=	jānā	=	to go
खाना	=	Khānā	=	to eat
दौड़ना	=	dauḍnā	=	to run
हँसना	=	hán'sánā	=	to Laugh

But the SECOND type of Hindi verbs, consist of TWO WORDS, i.e., a MAIN word followed by an ACCESSORY one:

To kill	=	mār ḍālánā	=	मार डालना
To wait	=	intezar káránā	=	इन्तजार करना
To bid	=	dāon' lágānā	=	दांव लगाना
To look (passive)	=	dikhāyee dénā	=	दिखायी देना
To faint	=	béhosh honā	=	बेहोश होना

To donate = *dān dénā* = दान देना

To remind = *yād dilānā* = याद दिलाना

When these words are used in sentences, only the accessory word undergoes changes according to the tense and the subject; the main word remains unchanges:

To kill : *mār ḍālā – mār ḍālé – mār ḍāléga.*

To faint : *behosh ho – behosh ho – behosh ho*
gáyā   gáyé   jayé gā

Now, an appropriately chosen adequate collection of Hindi verbs is being given which will be almost sufficient for the reader to form a variety of sentences while in this country.

The verbs are, of course, in alphabetical order.

1. To abscond   =   *Lāpátā honā*   =   लापता होना

2. To absorb   =   *Sokhánā*   =   सोखना

3.	To accept	=	Sweekār Káránā	=	स्वीकार करना
4.	To accompany	=	Sāth dénā	=	साथ देना
5.	To act	=	Káránā	=	करना
6.	To add	=	joḍánā	=	जोड़ना
7.	To admire	=	Práshánsā	=	प्रशंसा करना
8.	To advise	=	Sálāh dénā	=	सलाह देना
9.	To agree	=	Sáhmát honā	=	सहमत होना
10.	To allow	=	Anumati denā	=	अनुमति देना
11.	To annoy	=	Krodhit kármā	=	क्रोधित करना
12.	To apologize	=	Kshmā māngnā	=	क्षमा माँगना
13.	To apply	=	āvedán kármā	=	आवेदन करना
14.	To approach	=	Najdeek ānā	=	नजदीक आना
15.	To arise	=	Uthnā	=	उठना

16.	To arrange	=	*Vyávásthā Kárnā*	= व्यवस्था करना
17.	To arrive	=	*Páhunchānā*	= पहुँचाना
18.	To ask	=	*Poochhānā*	= पूछना
19.	To assist	=	*Sáhāyátā Kárnā*	= सहायता करना
20.	To assure	=	*āshwástá Kárnā*	= आश्वस्त करना
21.	To attach	=	*Joṛnā*	= जोड़ना
22.	To attack	=	*Ākrámán kárnā*	= आक्रमण करना
23.	To attempt	=	*Práyās Kárnā*	= प्रयास करना
24.	To attend	=	*Upásthit Ráhánā*	= उपस्थित रहना
25.	To attract	=	*ākárshit kárnā*	= आकर्षित करना
26.	To authorise	=	*adhikrut kármā*	= अधिकृत करना
27.	To awake	=	*Jāgnā*	= जगना
28.	To bake	=	*Pákānā*	= पकाना

29.	To ban	=	Pratibandh lágānā	= प्रतिबंध लगाना
30.	To bargein	=	molébhāw kárnā	= मोलभाव करना
31.	To bath	=	náhānā	= नहाना
32.	To batter	=	Peeṭánā	= पीटना
33.	To beat	=	Peeṭánā	= पीटना
34.	To befriend	=	mitrá bánānā	= मित्र बनाना
35.	To beg	=	bheekh māngánā	= भीख माँगना
36.	To begin	=	ārámbh kárnā	= आरंभ करना
37.	To behave	=	Vyáwhār kárnā	= व्यवहार करना
38.	To believe	=	Vishwās kárnā	= विश्वास करना
39.	To bend	=	moṛánā	= मोड़ना
40.	To betray	=	dhokhā dénā	= धोखा देना
41.	To bid	=	Kharidáné ké liyé dāoní lágānā	

खरीदने के लिए दाँव लगाना =

42.	To bite	=	*daant sé kātṇā*	=	दाँत से काटना
43.	To blast	=	*visphoṭe kárnā*	=	विस्फोट करना
44.	To bless	=	*āshirvād denā*	=	आशीर्वाद देना
45.	To block	=	*roké denā*	=	रोक देना
46.	To blossom	=	*Khilánā*	=	खिलना
47.	To blow	=	*Phoonkánā*	=	फूँकना
48.	To bolt	=	*band káranā*	=	बन्द करना
49.	To bore	=	*Chhéd káránā*	=	बन्द करना
50.	To bounce	=	*Uchhālánā*	=	उछालना
51.	To break	=	*Todánā*	=	तोड़ना
52.	To breath	=	*Saans lénā*	=	साँस लेना
53.	To brush	=	*Brush káráñā*	=	ब्रश करना

54.	To buy	=	*Kháridánā*	=	खरीदना
55.	To calculate	=	*Gándánā kárnā*	=	गणना करना
56.	To call	=	*Pukāránā*	=	पुकारना
57.	To cancel	=	*Nirást káránā*	=	निरस्त करना
58.	To care	=	*Dekhbhāl káránā*	=	देखभाल करना
59.	To carry	=	*Dhonā*	=	ढोना
60.	To cash	=	*Cash káránā*	=	कैश करना
61.	To catch	=	*Pákád lenā*	=	पकड़ लेना
62.	To certify	=	*Pr'amānit káránā*	=	प्रमाणित करना
63.	To change	=	*Bádálánā*	=	बदलना
64.	To chase	=	*Peechhā kárnā*	=	पीछा करना
65.	To cheat	=	*Thágénā*	=	ठगना
66.	To check	=	*Rokánā*	=	रोकना

67.	To choke	=	*Sāns ghutánā*	=	सांस घुटना
68.	To chop	=	*Tukádoń mein kātnā*	=	टुकड़ों में काटना
69.	To choose	=	*Chunánā*	=	चुनना
70.	To chuckle	=	*Khilkhilānā*	=	खिलखिलाना
71.	To circulate	=	*Prásārit kárnā*	=	प्रसारित करना
72.	To claim	=	*Dāwā kárnā*	=	दावा करना
73.	To clap	=	*Tāli bájānā*	=	ताली बजाना
74.	To clean	=	*Sáf kárānā*	=	साफ करना
75.	To clerch	=	*Jor se Pákáránā*	=	जोर से पकड़ना
76.	To close	=	*Bánd káránā*	=	बन्द करना
77.	To collect	=	*Prāptá káránā*	=	प्राप्त करना
			Ekátrá káránā	=	एकत्र करना

78.	To combine	=	Jornā	=	जोड़ना
79.	To come	=	ānā	=	आना
80.	To compel	=	Majboor káránā	=	मजबूर करना
81.	To complain	=	Shikáyat káránā	=	शिकायत करना
82.	To confide	=	Ráhásyá bátānā	=	रहस्य बताना
83.	To confiom	=	Pr'amānit káránā	=	प्रमाणित करना
84.	To contain	=	Apne ánder rákhánā	=	अपने अन्दर रखना
85.	To control	=	Niyántrán káránā	=	नियंत्रण करना
86.	To cover	=	Dhákánā	=	ढँकना
87.	To cry	=	Cheekhánā	=	चीखना
88.	To cure	=	Beemāri theek honā	=	बीमारी ठीक होना
89.	To cut	=	Kátnā/Kátnā	=	काटना, कटना
90.	To damage	=	Nuksān páhuṅchānā	=	नुकसान पहुंचाना

91.	To dance	=	Náchánā	=	नाचना
92.	To dare	=	Himmat káránā	=	हिम्मत करना
93.	To decay	=	Náshtá honā	=	नष्ट होना
94.	To decide	=	Nirnay kárnā	=	निर्णय करना
95.	To declare	=	Ghoshit káranā	=	घोषित करना
96.	To deferd	=	Bachao kárnā	=	बचाव करना
97.	To dehydrate	=	Jál-rahit káránā	=	जल रहित करना
98.	To delay	=	Der káránā	=	देर करना
99.	To deliver	=	Dena, Páhuchānā	=	पहुंचाना
100.	To demand	=	Mang káránā	=	मांग करना
101.	To demolish	=	Náshtá Káránā	=	नष्ट करना
102.	To depart	=	Prásthānkáránā	=	प्रस्थान करना
103.	To describe	=	Vyákhyā káránā	=	व्याख्या करना

104.	To desire	=	*Chāhánā*	= चाहना
105.	To die	=	*Márnā*	= मरना
106.	To dig	=	*Khodánā*	= खोदना
107.	To dip	=	*Dubānā*	= डुबाना
108.	To disagree	=	*a'sáhámát honā*	= असहमत होना
109.	To discolour	=	*Ráng chod denā*	= रंग छोड़ देना
110.	To disinfect	=	*Kitánu Ráhit Kárnā*	= कीटाणु रहित करना
111.	To dislike	=	*Nápásánd kárnā*	= नापसन्द करना
112.	To display	=	*Prádárshán kárnā*	= प्रदर्शन करना
113.	To distribute	=	*Bāṇtánā*	= बाँटना
114.	To do	=	*Káránā*	= करना
115.	To donote	=	*Dān denā*	= दान देना
116.	To dream	=	*Sápáne dekhnā*	= सपने देखना

117.	To drink	=	*Peenā*	पीना
118.	To dribble	=	*Dhar bankar tapakanā*	धार बनकर टपकना
119.	To drop	=	*Girānā*	गिराना
120.	To dry	=	*Sukhanā*	सुखाना
121.	To dye	=	*Ráṅgánā*	रंगना
122.	To eat	=	*Khānā*	खाना
123.	To edvcate	=	*Shikhshā denā*	शिक्षा देना
124.	To elect	=	*Chunánā*	चुनना
125.	To embarrass	=	*Lajjit honā/kárnā*	लज्जित होना/करना
126.	To emigrate	=	*Desh chhoḍnā*	देश छोड़ना
127.	To encourage	=	*Protsáhán denā*	प्रोत्साहन देना
128.	To enjoy	=	*Ānánd lénā*	आनन्द लेना

129.	To enter	=	Právésh kárnā	=	प्रवेश करना
130.	To erase	=	Mitānā	=	मिटाना
131.	To err	=	Galatee kárnā	=	गलती करना
132.	To escape	=	Báchánā	=	बचना
133.	To exhibit	=	Prádárshit kárnā	=	प्रदर्शित करना
134.	To expedite	=	Kām mein téji kárnā=	काम में तेजी करना
135.	To Fail	=	Asáphál honā	=	असफल होना
136.	To Faint	=	Béhosh honā	=	बेहोश होना
137.	To Fall	=	Girnā	=	गिरना
138.	To Fasten	=	Bāndhānā	=	बाँधना
139.	To Fear	=	Dáránā	=	डरना
140.	To Feed	=	Khilānā	=	खिलाना
141.	To Fight	=	Ládnā	=	लड़ना

142.	To Filter	=	*Chhānānā*	=	छनना
143.	To Finish	=	*Khátám káránā*	=	खत्म करना
144.	To Flee	=	*Bhāg jānā*	=	भाग जाना
145.	To Flow	=	*Báhānā*	=	बहाना
146.	To Fly	=	*Uḍānā*	=	उड़ाना
147.	To Forfeit	=	*Jábtá ho jānā*	=	जब्त हो जाना
148.	To forget	=	*Bhool Jānā*	=	भूल जाना
149.	To forgive	=	*Māf káránā*	=	माफ़ करना
150.	To frighten	=	*Dárānā*	=	डराना
151.	To gamble	=	*Juā khelánā*	=	जुआ खेलना
152.	To get	=	*Pānā*	=	पाना
153.	To go	=	*Jānā*	=	जाना
154.	To guard	=	*Rákshā káránā*	=	रक्षा करना

155.	To guide	=	*Rāstā Dikhānā*	=	रास्ता दिखाना
156.	To hang	=	*Látákānā*	=	लटकाना
157.	To harm	=	*Nuksān Páhunchānā*	=	नुकसान पहुँचाना
158.	To hase	=	*Náfrát kárnā*	=	नफरत करना
159.	To heat	=	*Gárám káránā*	=	गरम करना
160.	To help	=	*Sáhāyátā kárnā*	=	सहायता करना
161.	To hesitate	=	*Sánkoch kárnā*	=	संकोच करना
162.	To hide	=	*Chhipānā*	=	छिपाना
163.	To hit	=	*Máránā*	=	मारना
164.	To hold	=	*Pákádánā*	=	पकड़ना
165.	To honour	=	*Sánmān denā*	=	सम्मान देना
166.	To hug	=	*Galé lágānā*	=	गले लगाना
167.	To hurt	=	*Choṭ Páhuṅchānā*	=	चोट पहुँचाना

168.	To hypnotise	*Sámmohit kárnā*	=	सम्मोहित करना
169.	To identify	*Páhchánánā*	=	पहचानना
170.	To ignore	*Andekhā kárnā*	=	अनदेखा करना
171.	To imagine	*Kálpánā kárnā*	=	कल्पना करना
172.	To import	*Āyāt kárnā*	=	आयात करना
173.	To improve	*Sudhārnā*	=	सुधारना
174.	To include	*Shāmil kárnā*	=	शामिल करना
175.	To indicate	*Eshārā kárnā*	=	इशारा करना
176.	To influence	*Prábhāwit kárnā*	=	प्रभावित करना
177.	To insist	*Jor dekár Māng kárnā*	=	जोर देकर मांग करना
178.	To insure	*Beema kárnā*	=	बीमा करना/कराना
179.	To interrupt	*Bādhā dālnā*	=	बाधा डालना
180.	To intimate	*Soochit kárnā*	=	सूचित करना

181.	To introduce	=	*Prastut kárná* = प्रस्तुत करना
182.	To irrigate	=	*Seencháná* = सींचना
183.	To Join	=	*Jorná* = जोड़ना
184.	To joke	=	*Máják kárná* = मजाक करना
185.	To judge	=	*Nyáy kárná/Nirnay karná* न्याय करना/निर्णय करना
186.	To jump	=	*Kudáná* = कूदना
187.	To keep	=	*Rákhná* = रखना
188.	To kiss	=	*Chumáná* = चुम्ना
189.	To kneel	=	*Gnutáno per jhukáná* = घुट्नों पर झुकना
190.	To knock	=	*Dárwájá khátkhtáná* = दरवाजा खटखटाना
191.	To know	=	*Jánáná* = जानना
192.	To lack	=	*Maujudh Náhiń Honá* = मौजूद नहीं होना

193.	To land	=	*Jámeen pár utárná*	=	जमीन पर उतरना
194.	To laugh	=	*Hánsáná*	=	हंसना
195.	To Lay	=	*Rákhná*	=	रखना
196.	To lead	=	*Rāstā dikhānā*	=	रास्ता दिखाना
197.	To leak	=	*Dravya/Gas Nikālána*	=	द्रव्य या गैस निकालना
198.	To leap	=	*Kudáná*	=	कूदना
199.	To leave	=	*Chod denā*	=	छोड़ देना
200.	To lecture	=	*Bhāshán dénā*	=	भाषण देना
201.	To lend	=	*Udhār denā*	=	उधार देना
202.	To lift	=	*Uthānā*	=	उठाना
203.	To like	=	*Pásánd kárná*	=	पसन्द करना
204.	To live	=	*Jeetā Ráhāná*	=	जीता रहना
205.	To look	=	*Dhekhánā*	=	देखना

206.	To loosen	=	Dheelā kárnā	=	ढीला करना
207.	To love	=	Prem kárnā	=	प्रेम करना
208.	To lubricate	=	Geelā kárnā	=	गीला करना
209.	To mail	=	dāk se bhejánā	=	डाक से भेजना
210.	To make	=	Bánānā	=	बनाना
211.	To maltreat	=	Burā vyávāhār kárnā	=	बुरा व्यवहार करना
212.	To marry	=	Shādi kárnā	=	शादी करना
213.	To mash	=	Kuchálnā	=	कुचलना
214.	To massage	=	Mālish kárnā	=	मालिश करना
215.	To measure	=	Nāpánā	=	नापना
216.	To meet	=	Milánā	=	मिलना
217.	To misguide	=	Gálát Rāsta Bátānā	=	

218.	To miss	*Chhuṭ jānā* = छूट जाना	गलत रास्ता बताना =
219.	To misunderstand	*Gálát sámjhánā* = गलत समझना	
220.	To mix	*Milānā* = मिलाना	
221.	To nag	*Jid kárnā* = जिद करना	
222.	To nap	*Thodi dher sonā* = थोड़ी देर सोना	
223.	To need	*Járurhát Máhsus kárnā* = जरूरत महसूस करना	
224.	To notify	*Suchánā denā* = सूचना देना	
225.	To obey	*Mánánā* = मानना	
226.	To observe	*Dhyán denā* = ध्यान देना	
227.	To obtain	*Prāptá kárnā* = प्राप्त करना	
228.	To occupy	*Kábjā kárnā* = कब्जा करना	

229.	To offer	=	Pesh kárnā	=	पेश करना
230.	To ooze	=	Báhánā	=	बहना
231.	To open	=	Kholánā	=	खोलना
232.	To order	=	Aādhesh denā	=	आदेश देना
233.	To organize	=	Sángatthit kárnā	=	संगठित करना
234.	To overflow	=	Jyādhā Mātrā Main Báhánā	=	ज्यादा मात्रा में बहना
235.	To overload	=	Jyādhā Wáján Uthānā	=	ज्यादा वजन उठाना
236.	To overtake	=	Galát dháng se āge nikál jānā	=	गलत ढंग से आगे निकल जाना
237.	To own	=	Apne Adhikār Main Rákhánā	=	अपने अधिकार में रखना

238.	To Pacify	=	Shānt kárnā	=	शान्त करना
239.	To paint	=	Rángánā	=	रंगना
240.	To pass	=	Aāge Bádhánā	=	आगे बढ़ना
241.	To pay	=	Paisā denā	=	पैसा देना
242.	To peal	=	Chhilánā	=	छीलना
243.	To persuade	=	Sámjhānā	=	समझाना
244.	To play	=	Khelánā, Abhinay kárnā, Koi Vadyá yántrá Bajana	=	खेलना, अभिनय करना, कोई वाद्य यंत्र बजाना।
245.	To plead	=	Bār-Bār Anurodh Kárnā	=	बार-बार अनुरोध करना
246.	To popularize	=	Lokpriyá Bánānā	=	लोकप्रिय बनाना
247.	To post pone	=	Ţālánā	=	टालना
248.	To practise	=	Abhyās kárnā	=	अभ्यास करना

249.	To pray	=	Prārthánā kárnā	=	प्रार्थना करना
250.	To prepare	=	Taiyār kárnā	=	तैयार करना
251.	To pressurize	=	Dábāwá denā	=	दबाव देना
252.	To prevent	=	Rokánā	=	रोकना
253.	To prick	=	Chhedánā	=	छेदना
254.	To produce	=	Paidhā kárnā	=	पैदा करना
255.	To prolong	=	Bárhā denā	=	बढ़ा देना
256.	To prove	=	Prámānit kárnā	=	प्रमाणित करना
257.	To provoke	=	Uksānā	=	उकसाना
258.	To punish	=	Sájā denā	=	सजा देना
259.	To purshase	=	Kháridnā	=	खरीदना
260.	To push	=	Dhakelánā	=	ढकेलना
261.	To qualify	=	Kābil Honā	=	काबिल होना

262.	To quarrel	=	*Jhágárā kárnā*	झगड़ा करना
263.	To question	=	*Sáwāl kárnā*	सवाल करना
264.	To quit	=	*Jágáh chhod denā*	जगह छोड़ देना
265.	To rain	=	*Bārish Honā*	बारिश होना
266.	To reach	=	*Páhunchánā*	पहुंचना
267.	To read	=	*Pádhānā*	पढ़ना
268.	To re commend	=	*Siphārish kárnā*	सिफारिश करना
269.	To reduce	=	*Kām kárnā*	कम करना
270.	To regret	=	*Awásár khone ke bādh Afsos kárnā*	अवसर खोने के बाद अफसोस करना
271.	To reject	=	*Ashwiikar kárnā*	अस्वीकार करना
272.	To relax	=	*Aārām kárnā*	आराम करना
273.	To relieve	=	*Kásht kám kárnā*	कष्ट कम करना

274.	To repair	=	Maŕámmát kárnā	=	मरम्मत करना
275.	To repeat	=	Dhuhrānā	=	दुहराना
276.	To reply	=	Uttár denā	=	उत्तर देना
277.	To report	=	Ek likhit yā maukhik vivárán dénā	=	एक लिखित या मौखिक विवरण देना
278.	To rescue	=	Sánkáṭ sé Báchānā	=	संकट से बचाना
279.	To rest	=	Aārām kárnā	=	आराम करना
280.	To return	=	Lautānā	=	लौटना
281.	To ride	=	Sáwāri Kárnā	=	सवारी करना
282.	To rise	=	Uthānā	=	उठना
283.	To roar	=	Dháhāḍṇā	=	दहाड़ना
284.	To roast	=	Bhunānā	=	भूनना
285.	To rub	=	Ghisánā	=	घिसना

286.	To run	=	*Daudánā*	=	दौड़ना
287.	To rush	=	*Téji sé jānā*	=	तेजी से जाना
288.	To sacrifice	=	*Bálidhān kárnā*	=	बलिदान करना
289.	To sanction	=	*Anumati denā*	=	अनुमति देना
290.	To satisfy	=	*Sántust kárnā*	=	सन्तुष्ट करना
291.	To save	=	*Báchānā*	=	बचाना
292.	To say	=	*Káhnā*	=	कहना
293.	To scatter	=	*Bikhárā dena*	=	बिखरा देना
294.	To scratch	=	*Khujlānā, Khárochānā*	=	खुजलाना, खरोंचना
295.	To scream	=	*Chikhánā*	=	चीखना
296.	To search	=	*Khojánā*	=	खोजना
297.	To see	=	*Dhekhnā*	=	देखना
298.	To seek	=	*Khojánā*	=	खोजना

299.	To sell	=	Bechánā	=	बेचना
300.	To select	=	Chunánā	=	चुनना
301.	To separate	=	Aálég kárnā	=	अलग करना
302.	To shake	=	Hilānā	=	हिलाना
303.	To share	=	Hissā Lenā	=	हिस्सा लेना
304.	To shattu	=	Toḍánā	=	तोड़ना
305.	To shrink	=	Sikuḍánā	=	सिकुड़ना
306.	To shut	=	Bándh káránā	=	बन्द करना
307.	To sing	=	Gānā	=	गाना
308.	To sink	=	Ḍubánā	=	डूबना
309.	To sit	=	Baithánā	=	बैठना
310.	To slap	=	Jhāpáḍ Márnā	=	झापड़ मारना
311.	To sleep	=	sonā	=	सोना

312.	To slip	Fisálnā	=	फिसलना
313.	To smell	Sunghánā	=	सूंघना
314.	To snatch	Chhinánā	=	छीनना
315.	To speak	Bolánā	=	बोलना
316.	To spit	Thukánā	=	थूकना
317.	To spoil	Nashṭ kárnā	=	नष्ट करना
318.	To spray	Chhidákanā	=	छिड़कना
319.	To spread	Failānā	=	फैलाना
320.	To stab	Chāku mārnā	=	चाकू मारना
321.	To stain	Dāg lág jānā	=	दाग लग जाना
322.	To stand	Khaḍe Honā	=	खड़े होना
323.	To stare	Ghuránā	=	घूरना
324.	To start	Shuru kárnā	=	शुरू करना

325.	To stay	*Ṭhaháránā* =	ठहरना
326.	To steal	*Churānā* =	चुराना
327.	To stop	*Rokánā* =	रोकना
328.	To store	*Ikáthhā kárnā* =	इकट्ठा करना
329.	To stretch	*Failánā* =	फैलना
330.	To suck	*Chusánā* =	चूसना
331.	To suffer	*Kaṣṭ Sahánā* =	कष्ट सहना
332.	To surprise	*Chákit Honā/karnā* =	चकित होना/करना
333.	To surrerder	*Sámárrpán kárnā* =	समर्पण करना
334.	To swell	*Phool jaanā* =	फूल जाना
335.	To tackle	*Nipátánā* =	निपटना
336.	To tag	*Lágānā* =	लगाना
337.	To take	*Lenā* =	लेना

338.	To talk	=	*Bātá kárnā*	= बात करना
339.	To tap	=	*Ṭhákṭhkānā*	= ठकठकाना
340.	To tape	=	*Tape chipkānā*	= टेप चिपकाना
341.	To tatto	=	*Godwanā*	= गोदवाना
342.	To teach	=	*Sikhánā*	= सिखाना
343.	To tear	=	*Fāḍánā*	= फाड़ना
344.	To terrorise	=	*Aatánkit kárnā*	= आतंकित करना
345.	To testify	=	*Gáwāhi denā*	= गवाही देना
346.	To thank	=	*Dhānyawād denā*	= धन्यवाद देना
347.	To think	=	*Soachánā*	= सोचना
348.	To throw	=	*Fékánā*	= फेंकना
349.	To tie	=	*Bāndhnā*	= बांधना
350.	To tolerate	=	*Sahánā*	= सहना

351.	To torture	=	Kasht denā	=	कष्ट देना
352.	To touch	=	Chhunā	=	छूना
353.	To translate	=	Anuwadh kárnā	=	अनुवाद करना
354.	To tremble	=	Karípánā	=	कांपना
355.	To trim	=	Chhatánā	=	छांटना
356.	To trust	=	Bishwās karnā	=	विश्वास करना
357.	To try	=	Koshish kárnā	=	कोशिश करना
358.	To turn	=	Mundnā	=	मुड़ना
359.	To type	=	Type kárnā	=	टाइप करना
360.	To understand	=	Samjhánā	=	समझना
361.	To undress	=	Kapḍa utārnā	=	कपड़ा उतारना
362.	To unite	=	Sángáthit Honā	=	संगठित होना
363.	To unload	=	Gaḍi se sāmān utāranā	=	गाड़ी से समान उतारना

364.	To unlock	=	Talā kholánā	=	ताला खोलना
365.	To upset	=	Páreshān kárnā/Honā	=	परेशान करना/होना
366.	To use	=	Upáyog karnā	=	उपयोग करना
367.	To vacate	=	Jágáh khāli kárnā	=	जगह खाली करना
368.	To vary	=	Fárk Honā	=	फर्क होना
369.	To violate	=	Bháng kárnā	=	भंग करना
370.	To vote	=	Mát denā	=	मत देना
371.	To wait	=	Intjar kárnā	=	इन्तजार करना
372.	To wake	=	Jāgánā	=	जागना
373.	To walk	=	Chálánā, Táhálnā	=	चलना, टहलना
374.	To wander	=	Idhár, Udhár Ghumánā	=	इधर-उधर घूमना

375.	To warm	=	Gárm kárnā	=	गर्म करना
376.	To wash	=	Dhonā	=	धोना
377.	To waste	=	Barbadh karnā	=	बरबाद करना
378.	To watch	=	Dhyān se dekhánā	=	ध्यान से देखना
379.	To wave	=	Hilanā	=	हिलाना
380.	To weigh	=	Taulánā	=	तौलना
381.	To whip	=	Koḍā Marnā	=	कोड़ा मारना
382.	To whisper	=	Fusfusānā	=	फुसफुसाना
383.	To whistle	=	Citee Bajanā	=	सीटी बजाना
384.	To wink	=	Aankh Marnā	=	आंख मारना
385.	To withdraw	=	Vāpás lenā	=	वापस लेना
386.	To work	=	Kām karnā	=	काम करना
387.	To worry	=	Chintā karnā	=	चिन्ता करना
388.	To write	=	Likhánā	=	लिखना

Nouns

1. Account = *Khātā* = खाता
2. Acid = *amlá* = अम्ल
3. Actor = *abhinétā* = अभिनेता
4. Address = *pátā* = पता
5. Advertisement = *vigyāpán* = विज्ञापन
6. Agriculture = *khétee* = खेती
7. Anger = *krodh* = क्रोध
8. Animal = *jānwár* = जानवर
9. Ankle = *ṭákhánā* = टखना
10. Answer = *jáwāb* = जवाब
11. Apology = *kshámā* = क्षमायाचना
    yāchánā
12. Arch = *méhrāb* = मेहराब
13. Arm = *bān'h* = बांह

14.	Armpit	= *kān'kh*	=	कांख
15.	Baby	= *báchchā*	=	बच्चा
16.	Bachelor	= *kun'wārā*	=	कुवांरा
17.	Back	= *peeṭh*	=	पीठ
18.	Backbone	= *méru dáṇḍ*	=	मेरूदण्ड़
19.	Backyárd	= *pichhwāḍā*	=	पिछवाड़ा
20.	Bananā	= *kelā*	=	केला
21.	Beard	= *dāḍhee*	=	दाढ़ी
22.	Bed	= *bistār*	=	बिस्तर
23.	Blister	= *phápholá*	=	फफोला
24.	Blood	= *khoon*	=	खून
25.	Belly	= *pét*	=	पेट
26.	Book	= *kitāb*	=	किताब
27.	Boy	= *Láḍkā*	=	लड़का
28.	Brain	= *dimāg*	=	दिमाग
29.	Bride	= *dulhán*	=	दुल्हन
30.	Bug	= *keeḍā*	=	कीड़ा
31.	Butter	= *mákkhán*	=	मक्खन
32.	Cabbage	= *páttā gobhee*	=	पत्ता गोभी
33.	Calf	= *báchhádā*	=	बछड़ा

34. Camel	= *Oon't*	= ऊंट
35. Cap	= *Topee*	= टोपी
36. Carpet	= *kāleen*	= कालीन
37. Carrot	= *gājár*	= गाजर
38. Chair	= *kursee*	= कुर्सी
39. Chamaleon	= *girgiṭ*	= गिरगिट
40. Cheek	= *gāl*	= गाल
41. Chest	= *Chhātee*	= छाती
42. Citizen	= *nāgárik*	= नागरिक
43. Coal	= *koylā*	= कोयला
44. Coast	= *samudrá ka kinārā*	
	= समुद्र का किनारा	
45. Coin	= *Sikkā*	= सिक्का
46. Colour	= *ráng*	= रंग
47. Corner	= *konā*	= कोना
48. Coward	= *kāyár*	= कायर
49. Cow	= *Gai*	= गाय
50. Crime	= *apárādh*	= अपराध
51. Crop	= *fásál*	= फसल
52. Crow	= *kauwā*	= कौवा

53. Crown	= *mukuṭ*	= मुकुट
54. Custody	= *hirāsát*	= हिरासत
55. Dance	= *nāch*	= नाच
56. Danger	= *khátárā*	= खतरा
57. Date	= *tāreekh*	= तारीख
58. Day	= *din*	= दिन
59. Death	= *maut*	= मौत
60. Decoration	= *sájāwáṭ*	= सजावट
61. Deer	= *hirán*	= हिरन
62. Department	= *vibhāg*	= विभाग
63. Desert	= *régistān*	= रेगिस्तान
64. Dog	= *kuttā*	= कुत्ता
65. Door	= *dárwājā*	= दरवाजा
66. Doubt	= *sándeh*	= सन्देह
67. Dozen	= *darjan*	= दर्जन
68. Dream	= *sápánā*	= सपना
69. Dress	= *poshāk*	= पोशाक
70. Drink	= *péyá*	= पेय
71. Drop	= *boond*	= बून्द
72. Duck	= *báttákh*	= बत्तख

73.	Dumb	= goongā	= गूंगा
74.	Dust	= dhool	= धूल
75.	Eagle	= cheel	= चील
76.	Ear	= kān	= कान
77.	Earth	= prithwi	= पृथ्वी
78.	East	= poorab	= पूरब
79.	Echo	= pratidhwáni	= प्रतिध्वनि
80.	Economy	= arth vyāwásthā	
		= अर्थ व्यवस्था	
81.	Editor	= sámpādak	= सम्पादक
82.	Education	= shikshā	= शिक्षा
83.	Eclipse	= gráhán	= ग्रहण
84.	Elbow	= kuhánee	= कुहनी
85.	End	= antá	= अन्त
86.	Energy	= oorjá	= ऊर्जा
87.	Environment	= vatāvárán	= वातावरण
88.	Event	= ghátánā	= घटना
89.	Eye	= ānkh	= आंख
90.	Eye brow	= bhaun'	= भौं
91.	Eye lashes	= palakén	= पलकें

92.	Eye witness	= *gáwāh*	= गवाह
93.	Face	= *chehárā*	= चेहरा
94.	Fair	= *melā*	= मेला
95.	Fan	= *pánkhā*	= पंखा
96.	Farm	= *khét*	= खेत
97.	Father	= *pitā*	= पिता
98.	Fire	= *āg*	= आग
99.	Finger	= *unglee*	= अंगुली
100.	Fish	= *máchhalee*	= मछली
101.	Flag	= *jhándā*	= झण्डा
102.	Flame	= *jwālā*	= ज्वाला
103.	Flesh	= *mān's*	= मांस
104.	Fly	= *mākkhee*	= मक्खी
105.	Floor	= *fárshá*	= फर्श
106.	Flour	= *āṭā*	= आटा
107.	Flower	= *phool*	= फूल
108.	Flower pot	= *Gul dástā*	= गुलदस्ता
109.	Flute	= *bānsuree*	= बांसुरी
110.	Foam	= *jhāg*	= झाग
111.	Fog	= *kohrā*	= कोहरा

112. Foot	= *pan'w*	= पांव
113. Forehead	= *māṭhā*	= माथा
114. Fort	= *kilā*	= किला
115. Fountain	= *pháwwārā*	= फव्वारा
116. Frog	= *medhák*	= मेढ़क
117. Fuel	= *indhán*	= ईंधन
118. Function	= *utsáv*	= उत्सव
119. Future	= *bhávishyá*	= भविष्य
120. Gamble	= *juā*	= जुआ
121. Garbage	= *kooḍā*	= कूड़ा
122. Garden	= *bāg*	= बाग
123. Girl	= *láḍkee*	= लड़की
124. Glass	= *sheeshā*	= शीशा
	gilās	= गिलास
125. Glove	= *dástānā*	= दस्ताना
126. Glue	= *gond*	= गोंद
127. Goat	= *bákáree*	= बकरी
128. God	= *eeshwár*	= ईश्वर
129. Gold	= *sonā*	= सोना
130. Grand father	= *dādā*	= दादा

131.	Grand mother	=	*dādee*	= दादी
132.	Grape	=	*angoor*	= अंगूर
133.	Grave	=	*kábrá*	= कब्र
134.	Guard	=	*rakshak*	= रक्षक
135.	Guest	=	*mehmān*	= मेहमान
136.	Gum	=	*msooḍā*	= मसूड़ा
137.	Habit	=	*ādát*	= आदत
138.	Hair	=	*bāl*	= बाल
139.	Haj	=	*haj*	= हज
140.	Hand	=	*Hāth*	= हाथ
141.	Hammer	=	*háthaudā*	= हथौड़ा
142.	Hazard	=	*khátárā*	= ख़तरा
143.	Head	=	*sir*	= सिर
144.	Heap	=	*ḍhér*	= ढेर
145.	Heart	=	*hridáyá*	= हृदय
146.	Heat	=	*gármee*	= गर्मी
147.	Heel	=	*éḍee*	= एड़ी
148.	Hip	=	*koolhā*	= कूल्हा
149.	History	=	*Itihās*	= इतिहास
150.	Hole	=	*chhed*	= छेद

151. Home	= *ghár*	= घर
152. Honey	= *sháhád*	= शहद
153. Horn	= *seeng*	= सींग
154. Horse	= *ghoḍā*	= घोड़ा
155. Hour	= *ghánṭā*	= घन्टा
156. Husband	= *páti*	= पति
157. Hypnosis	= *sammohán*	= सम्मोहन
158. Importance	= *máhátwá*	= महत्व
159. Industrial	= *audyogik*	= औद्योगिक
160. Information	= *soochánā*	= सूचना
161. Jewellery	= *gáhánā*	= गहना
162. Joke	= *májāk*	= मजाक
163. Judgement	= *faisálā*	= फ़ैसला
164. Key	= *chābi*	= चाबी
165. Knife	= *chākoo*	= चाकू
166. Knot	= *gānṭh*	= गांठ
167. Knee	= *ghuṭnā*	= घुटना
168. Knowledge	= *jānkāree*	= जानकारी
169. Laboratory	= *práyogshālā*	= प्रयोगशाला
170. Lad	= *chhokárā*	= छोकरा

171. Lady	= *mahilā*	= महिला
172. Lamb	= *mémánā*	= मेमना
173. Land	= *bhumi*	= भूमि
174. Lane	= *gálee*	= गली
175. Language	= *bhāshā*	= भाषा
176. Lap	= *god*	= गोद
177. Laughter	= *hánsee*	= हंसी
178. Law	= *kānoon*	= कानून
179. Leaf	= *pattee*	= पत्ती
180. Leather	= *chamaḍā*	= चमड़ा
181. Leopard	= *ténduā*	= तेंदुआ
182. Lemon	= *neen'boo*	= नींबू
183. Lettuce	= *pālák*	= पालक
184. Life	= *jeeván*	= जीवन
185. Leg	= *pair*	= पैर
186. Lip	= *honṭh*	= होंठ
187. Literature	= *sāhityá*	= साहित्य
188. Lock	= *tālā*	= ताला
189. Lotus	= *kámál*	= कमल
190. Love	= *pyār*	= प्यार

191.	Lover	= *prémee*	= प्रेमी
192.	Lunch	= *din kā khānā*	
		= दिन का खाना	
193.	Lung	= *phephḍā*	= फेफड़ा
194.	Magic	= *jādoo*	= जादू
195.	Magnet	= *chumbák*	= चुम्बक
196.	Maid	= *naukárānee*	= नौकरानी
197.	Majority	= *báhumát*	= बहुमत
198.	Man	= *ādámee*	= आदमी
199.	Map	= *nákshā*	= नक्शा
200.	Massage	= *mālish*	= मालिश
201.	Material	= *sāmágree*	= सामग्री
202.	Meal	= *khānā*	= खाना
203.	Medicine	= *dáwā*	= दवा
204.	Melon	= *tárbooj*	= तरबूज
205.	Mind	= *dimāg*	= दिमाग
206.	Mirror	= *dárpán*	= दर्पण
207.	Monument	= *smārák*	= स्मारक
208.	Mosquito	= *máchhár*	= मच्छर
209.	Mother	= *mān'*	= मां

210.	Murder	= *hátyā*	= हत्या
211.	Mustache	= *moońchh*	= मूंछ
212.	Mustard	= *sáráson'*	= सरसों
213.	Mystery	= *ráhásyá*	= रहस्य
214.	Name	= *nām*	= नाम
215.	Nationality	= *rāshtreeyátā*	= राष्ट्रीयता
216.	Nature	= *prákriti*	= प्रकृति
217.	Need	= *zaroorát*	= जरूरत
218.	Needle	= *sooee*	= सूई
219.	Neighbour	= *paḍosee*	= पड़ोसी
220.	Nest	= *ghońsálā*	= घोंसला
221.	News	= *sámāchār*	= समाचार
222.	Night	= *rāt*	= रात
223.	Nose	= *nāk*	= नाक
224.	Neck	= *gárdán*	= गर्दन
225.	Nail	= *nākhoon*	= नाखून
226.	Onion	= *pyāz*	= प्याज़
227.	Owl	= *ulloo*	= उल्लू
228.	Pain	= *dárd*	= दर्द
229.	Palm	= *hathelee*	= हथेली

230.	Parrot	= totā	= तोता
231.	Patient	= rogee	= रोगी
232.	Peacock	= mor	= मोर
233.	People	= log	= लोग
234.	Pepper	= mirchá	= मिर्च
235.	Person	= vyákti	= व्यक्ति
236.	Pillow	= takiyā	= तकिया
237.	Place	= sthān	= स्थान
238.	Poison	= záhár	= ज़हर
239.	Population	= ābādee	= आबादी
240.	Pot	= bártán	= बर्तन
241.	Potato	= āloo	= आलू
242.	Prayer	= prārthánā	= प्रार्थना
243.	Price	= keemát	= कीमत
244.	Prize	= puráskār	= पुरस्कार
245.	Prince	= rājkumār	= राजकुमार
246.	Princess	= rajkumāri	= राजकुमारी
247.	Queen	= rānee	= रानी
248.	Question	= práshná	= प्रश्न
249.	Rabbit	= khárgosh	= खरगोश

250.	Race	= *dauḍ*	= दौड़
251.	Reason	= *kārán*	= कारण
252.	Refugee	= *sháráṇārthee*	= शरणार्थी
253.	Residence	= *niwās*	= निवास
254.	River	= *nádee*	= नदी
255.	Rock	= *cháṭṭān*	= चट्टान
256.	Roof	= *chhát*	= छत
257.	Root	= *jáḍ*	= जड़
258.	Rose	= *gulāb*	= गुलाब
259.	Sacred	= *pavitrá*	= पवित्र
260.	Salary	= *vétán*	= वेतन
261.	Salt	= *námák*	= नमक
262.	Sand	= *bāloo*	= बालू
263.	Scorpion	= *bichhoo*	= बिच्छू
264.	Season	= *mausám*	= मौसम
265.	She	= *woh*	= वह
266.	Sheet	= *chādár*	= चादर
267.	Song	= *geet*	= गीत
268.	Skin	= *khāl*	= खाल
269.	Sky	= *ākāsh*	= आकाश

270.	Slap	= *jhāpáḍ*	=	झापड़
271.	Snake	= *sān'p*	=	सांप
272.	Society	= *sámāj*	=	समाज
273.	South	= *dakshin*	=	दक्षिण
274.	Spoon	= *chámmách*	=	चम्मच
275.	Thing	= *cheez*	=	चीज़
276.	Thigh	= *jāngh*	=	जांघ
277.	Thousand	= *házār*	=	हज़ार
278.	Time	= *wáktá*	=	वक्त
279.	Toe	= *pair kee ungaliyān*
		= पैर की उंगलियां
280.	Tooth	= *dānt*	=	दांत
281.	Trade	= *vyāpār*	=	व्यापार
282.	Ultimatum	= *ākhiree chetāwánee*
		= आखिरी चेतावनी
283.	Umbrellā	= *chhātā*	=	छाता
284.	Vegetable	= *sábzee*	=	सब्ज़ी
285.	Vehicle	:= *gāḍee*	=	गाड़ी
286.	Village	= *gāon'*	=	गांव
287.	Violet	= *baigánee*	=	बैगनी

288.	Volcano	= *jwālāmukhee*	= ज्वालामुखी
289.	Waist	= *kámár*	= कमर
290.	Water	= *pānee*	= पानी
291.	Wave	= *láhár*	= लहर
292.	Wax	= *mom*	= मोम
293.	Weapon	= háthiyār	= हथियार
294.	Week	= sáptāh	= सप्ताह
295.	Weight	= wáján	= वजन
296.	West	= páschim	= पश्चिम
297.	Wheel	= páhiyā	= पहिया
298.	Wind	= háwā	= हवा
299.	Woman	= aurát	= औरत
300.	Word	= shábdá	= शब्द
301.	Work	= kām	= काम
302.	World	= duniyān	= दुनियां
303.	Worship	= poojā	= पूजा
304.	Year	= sāl	= साल
305.	Yesterday	= kál	= कल
306.	Youth	= jáwān	= जवान

Introduce yourself

1. I am British

   Main british hoon.

   (मैं ब्रिटिश हूँ.)

2. But I have US citizenship.

   Lékin méré pās ámériki nāgárikátā hai.

   (लेकिन मेरेपास अमेरिकी नागरिकता है.)

3. I have come from Singapore

   Main Singapore sé āyā hoon'.

   (मैं सिंगापोर से आया हूँ.)

4. Oh, my name is ....

   Oh, mera nām .... hai.

   (ओह मेरा नाम .... है.)

5. I am a teacher by profession.

   Péshé sé main ék shikshák hoon.

(पेशे से मैं एक शिक्षक हूँ.)

6. My hobbies are-travelling and writing.

   Méré shauk hain-yātrā káránā aur likhánā.

   (मेरे शौक हैं—यात्रा करना और लिखना.)

7. I have a passport valid upto ....

   Mere pās ék passport hai jiskee áwádhi .... tak hai.

   (मेरे पास एक पासपोर्ट है जिसकी अवधि .... तक है.)

8. My visa Lasts on ....

   Méra veeja .... tāreekh ko khátám hota hai.

   (मेरा वीजा .... तारीख को खत्म होता है.)

9. I am married.

   Main vivāhit hoon.

   (मैं विवाहित हूँ.)

10. No, my wife has not come with me.

    Naheen, meri pátnee méré sāth n'aheen āyee hai.

    (नहीं, मेरी पत्नी मेरे साथ नहीं आयी है.)

11. I have come alone.

    Main ákélā āyā hoon'.

    (मैं अकेला आया हूँ.)

12. I have never been to this country before.

    Main is desh mén páhálé kábhee náheen āyā hoon'.

    (मैं इस देश में पहले कभी नहीं आया हूँ.)

13. Along with MountAbu, I have to visit Jaipur also.

    MountAbu ke sāth sāth mujhe Jaipur bhi ghoománā hai.

    (माउन्ट आबु के साथ-साथ मुझे जयपुर भी घूमना है.)

14. I'll catch my flight back on ....

    *Main wāpásee kā ápnā jáhāj ....
    Ko pakaḍoongā.*

    (मैं वापसी का अपना जहाज .... को पकड़ूंगा.)

15. My height is 6ft. 2inches.

    Meri lámbāyee chhe foot do inch hai.

    (मेरी लम्बाई छे फुट दो इन्च है.)

16. My weight is 82 Kilograms.

Mérā wáján báyāsee kilo hai.

(मेरा वजन बयासी किलो है।)

17. I have got my suite booked at hotel Radisson.

Main hotel Radisson mén ápnā suite book kárā chuka hoon.

(मैं होटल रैडिसन में अपना सूट बुक करा चुका हूँ।)

18. I have visited almost the whole of Europe.

Main kareeb poorā Europe ghoom chuka hoon.

(मैं करीब पूरा यूरोप घूम चुका हूँ।)

19. I find hospitality of Indians really great.

Main Bhartiyon ki mehmānáwāzi ko sāchmuch máhān pātā hoon.

(मैं भारतीयों की मेहमानवाजी को सचमुच महान पाता हूँ।)

20. I prefer vegetarian food.

Main shākāhāree bhoján ko prathamikta détā hoon.

(मैं शाकाहारी भोजन को प्राथमिकता देता हूँ।)

21. I have a good camera.

    Méré pās ék achhā camera hai.

    (मेरे पास एक अच्छा कैमरा है.)

22. My luggage is light and simple.

    Mérā sāmān hálka aur sādhāráṇ hai.

    (मेरा सामान हल्का और साधारण है.)

23. I have not brought my laptop computer.

    Main ápnā laptop computer náheen lāyā hoon'.

    (मैं अपना लैपटॉप कम्प्यूटर नहीं लाया हूँ.)

24. I will take some books with me.

    Main ápné sāth kuchh kitabén lé jāoongā..

    (मैं अपने साथ कुछ किताबे ले जाऊंगा.)

25. I can give you this book free.

    Main āpáko yéh kitāb muftá mén dé sákátā hoon'.

    (मैं आपको यह किताब मुफ्त में दे सकता हूँ.)

At the customs

1. Do I have to fill up any papers?

   Kyā mujhé koee kāgzāt bháráne honge'?

   (क्या मुझे कोई कागज़ात भरने होंगे!)

2. Where do I sign?

   Mujhé dástákhát káhān káráné hain?

   (मुझे दस्तख़त कहां करने हैं?)

3. Yes, both these black bags are mine!

   Haan ye dono kāle bag méré hain!

   (हां, ये दोनों काले बैग मेरे हैं!)

4. No, that leather suitcase is not mine.

   Naheen, woh chámáḍé kā suitcase merā náheen hai.

   (नहीं, वह चमड़े का सूटकेस मेरा नहीं है।)

5. What do I have to declare?

Mujhe kyā declare karanā hoga?

(मुझे क्या डिक्लेयर करना होगा?)

6. Is this bottle of perfume dutiable?

   Kyā perfume kee is sheeshee pár kár lagégā?

   (क्या परफ्यूम की इस शीशी पर 'कर' लगेगा?)

7. Can I import this bottle of wine?

   Kyā main shárāb kee yeh bottle le jā sákátā hoon'?

   (क्या मैं शराब की यह बोतल ले जा सकता हूँ?)

8. Yes, this is my health certificate.

   Hān, yeh merā health certificate hai.

   (हाँ, यह मेरा हेल्थ सर्टीफिकेट है.)

9. These are my personal belongings?

   Yéh méré vyáktigát sāmān hain?

   (ये मेरे व्यक्तिगत सामान हैं.)

10. Do I have to open the bag?

    Kyā mujhé bag kholánā hoga?

    (क्या मुझे बैग खोलना होगा?)

11. Where is the toilet?

    Shauchāláyá káhān hai?

(शौचालय कहां है?)

12. Is there a coffee shop here?

Kyā yáhān coffee shop hai?

(क्या यहां कॉफी शॉप है?)

13. How can I reach Hotel Radisson?

Main hotel Radisson ták kaisé páhunch sákátā hoon'?

(मैं होटल रैडिसन तक कैसे पहुंच सकता हूँ?)

14. How far it is?

Yeh kitnee door hai?

(यह कितनी दूर है?)

15. Where can I get a taxi?

Mujhe taxi káhān milégee?

(मुझे टैक्सी कहाँ मिलेगी?)

16. Can I get Indian currency here?

Kyā mujhé yáhān Bhārátiyá mudrā mil sákátee hai?

(क्या मुझे यहाँ भारतीय मुद्रा मिल सकती है?)

17. Do you have traveller's cheques?

Kyā āpké pās traveller's cheques hain?

(क्या आपके पास ट्रैवेलर्स चेक्स है?)

18. Kindly give me the receipt.

    Kripáyā mujhé ráseed dijiyé.

    (कृपया मुझे रसीद दीजिये.)

19. How about these US made medicines?

    Amerika mén bánee in dáwāon' ke bāré mein āp kyā kahte hain?

    (अमेरिका में बनी इन दवाओं के बारे में आप क्या कहते है?)

20. They are for my personal use.

    Wé meré vyaktigát upáyog ké liyé haiń.

    (वे मेरे व्यक्तिगत उपयोग के लिये है.)

21. Thank god, that I can carry them.

    Ishwar ko dhányáwād ki main inhe lé jā sakata hoon'.

    (ईश्वर को धन्यवाद कि इन्हें मैं ले जा सकता हूँ.)

22. Well, kindly guide me to the exit.

    Theek hai, kripaya mujhe bāhár ka rāstā bátāiyé.

    (ठीक है, कृपया मुझे बाहर का रास्ता बताईये.)

23. Do you speak English?

   Kyā āp english bolāté hain?

   (क्या आप इंग्लिश बोलते है?)

24. Kindly explain my problem to the taxi driver.

   Kripáyā meri sámásyā taxi driver ko sámájhā dijiye.

   (कृपया मेरी समस्या टैक्सी ड्राइवर को समझा दीजिये।)

25. Is there a bus or train service to the city?

   Kyā sháhár ke liye koyee bus yā train séwā hai?

   (क्या शहर के लिये कोई बस या ट्रेन सेवा है?)

Conversation with taxi driver

1. Can you take me to hotel Radisson?

   Kyā tum mujhe hotel Radisson lé chál sákáte ho?

   (क्या तुम मुझे होटल रैडिसन ले चल सकते हो?)

2. Yes, I have got a booking there.

   Hān, wáhān páhále sé hee meri booking hai.

   (हाँ वहां पहले से ही मेरी बुकिंग है।)

3. How much will you charge?

   Tum kitnā paisa logé?

   (तुम कितना पैसा लोगे?)

4. Three hundred rupees are toò much.

   Teen sau rupayé bahut jyādāh hain.

   (तीन सौ रुपये बहुत ज्यादा है।)

5. I have seen the rate list.

Maine 'rate list' dékhā hai.

(मैंने रेट लिस्ट देखा है।)

6. Two hundred rupees are enough.

   Do sau rupáyé theek hain.

   (दो सौ रुपये ठीक हैं।)

7. O.K., you load this luggage.

   Theek hai, tum yeh sāmān r'akho.

   (ठीक है तुम यह सामान रखो।)

8. How long will it take to reach?

   Páhunchané mén kitnā wáktá lágégā?

   (पहुंचने में कितना वक्त लगेगा?)

9. Since when you are driving in this city?

   Káb sé tum is sháhár mén gādee chálā rahe ho?

   (कब से तुम इस शहर में गाड़ी चला रहे हो?)

10. Can I hire your taxi for a full day?

    Kyā main tumhāri taxi puré din ké liyé lé sákátā hoon'?

    (क्या मैं तुम्हारी टैक्सी पूरे दिन के लिये ले सकता हूँ?)

11. Will you charge on hourly basis?

Kyā tum ghánton' ké hisāb se charge logé?

(क्या तुम घन्टों के हिसाब से चार्ज लोगे?)

12. Or according to distance?

Yā doori ké hisāb se?

(या दूरी के हिसाब से?)

13. How can I contact you?

Main tumhén kaisé contact kár śakátā hoon?

(मैं तुम्हें कैसे कॉन्टैक्ट कर सकता हूँ?)

14. Well, we are almost there.

Achhā, áb hám páhunch chuké hain.

(अच्छा, हम अब पहुंच चुके हैं.)

15. Thank you for this interesting ride.

Is dilchásp yātrā ké liyé dhányawād!

(इस दिलचस्प यात्रा के लिये धन्यवाद!)

At the hotel

1. I hope I have got a reservation.

   Main āshā kárátā hoon' ki mere nām sé ýahān reservation hai.

   (मैं आशा करता हूँ कि मेरे नाम से यहां रिजर्वेशन है)

2. Yes, I asked for a single bed room

   Hān, mainé ék bed wāle room ké liyé káhā thā.

   (हां, मैंने एक बेड वाले रूम के लिये कहा था.)

3. I had wired from singapore.

   Mainé singapore sé tār bhéjā thā.

   (मैंने सिंगापोर से तार भेजा था.)

4. I sent it about a week ago.

   Mainé isé kareeb ék sáptāh páhále bhejā thā.

   (मैंने इसे करीब एक सप्ताह पहले भेजा था.)

5. Oh, thank god that I have got my room.

Oh, eeshwar ko dhányáwád ki mujhe mérā room mil gáyā hai.

(ओह ईश्वर को धन्यवाद कि मुझे मेरा रूम मिल गया है.)

6. No, I failed to wire you in advance.

   Náheen main advance mén āpké pās tār náheen dé s'akā.

   (नहीं मैं ऐडवान्स में आपके पास तार नहीं दे सका)

7. Kindly, try your best.

   Kɩipáyā pooree koshish kijiyé.

   (कृपया पूरी कोशिश कीजिये)

8. O.K., a double bed room will do.

   Theek hai, ék double-bed-room bhee chalega.

   (ठीक है, एक डबल बेडरूम भी चलेगा)

9. How much will it be?

   Iskā kirāyā kitnā hoga?

   (इसका किराया कितना होगा?)

10. Quite reasonable.

    Kāfee uchit hai.

    (काफी उचित है.)

11.   Oh, it's quite expensive.

  Oh, yeh kafee máhéngā hai.

  (ओह यह काफी महंगा है.)

12.   Does it include any meals.

  Kyā ismén koi khānā bhee shāmil hai.

  (क्या इसमें कोई खाना भी शामिल है.)

13.   I have to stay for three days.

  Mujhe teen din ṭháháránā hai.

  (मुझे तीन दिन ठहरना है.)

14.   No, for one night only.

  Naheen, sirf ék rāt ké liyé.

  (नहीं सिर्फ एक रात के लिये.)

15.   It is quite small.

  Yeh kāfee chhoṭā hai.

  (यह काफी छोटा है.)

16.   It is not cool.

  Yeh ṭhándā náheeń hai.

  (यह ठन्डा नहीं है.)

17.   The window does not face the sea.

  Yeh khiḍkee sámudrá ki táráf náheen hai.

  (यह खिड़की समुद्र की तरफ नहीं है.)

18. It doesn't appear adequately clean.

    Yáhān sáfāi páryāptá naheen hai.

    (यहां सफाई पर्याप्त नहीं है.)

19. Kindly clean it first.

    Kripáyā páhálé isé sāf káro.

    (कृपया पहले इसे साफ करो.)

20. How can I get some fresh air?

    Main kuchh tājee háwā kaisé pā sákátā hoon?

    (मैं कुछ ताजी हवा कैसे पा सकता हूँ?)

21. Do you have air conditioned rooms?

    Kyā āpke pās air conditioned room hain?

    (क्या आपके पास एयर कन्डीशन रूम हैं?)

22. What will be the extra charge?

    Iské liyé atiriktá charge kyā hogā?

    (इसके लिये अतिरिक्त चार्ज क्या होगा.)

23. Can I check out at 10.00 AM?

    Kyā main dás bájé subah hotel chhoḍ sákátā hoon?

    (क्या मैं दस बजे सुबह होटल छोड़ सकता हूँ?)

24. Is cre‌   ‌cility available?

Kyā credit card sweekār káráné ki suwidhā hai?

(क्या क्रेडिट कार्ड स्वीकार करने की सुविधा है?)

25. Does the bank have ATM facility?

Kyā is bank mén ATM suwidha hai?

(क्या इस बैंक में ATM सुविधा है?)

26. Where is my key?

Meree chābi káhān' hai?.

(मेरी चाबी कहां है?)

27. Here is my key.

Méree chābi yáhān hai.

(मेरी चाबी यहां है.)

28. No, I am a vegetarian.

Naheen, main shākāhāree hoon'.

(नहीं मैं शाकाहारी हूँ.)

29. I eat eggs.

Main anḍé khātā hoon'.

(मैं अन्डे खाता हूँ.)

30. Can I order wine in my room?

Kyā main apné room men shárāb order kár sákátā hooń?

(क्या मैं अपने रूम में शराब ऑर्डर कर सकता हूँ?)

31. Am I allowed to take my lady friends to my room?

Kyā mujhe apnee mahila mitron' ko apné room meń lé jāné ki anumáti hai ?

(क्या मुझे अपनी महिला मित्रों को अपने रूम में ले जाने की अनुमति है?)

32. What are the means of entertainment available here?

Yáhān manoranjan ke kaun sé sādhán hain?

(यहां मनोरंजन के कौन से साधन हैं?)

33. Hello reception, kindly connect me to phone number.......!

Hello reception, kripaya mujhe phonenumber.......... se connect kár dijiye!

(हेलो रिसेप्शन, कृपया मुझे फोन नम्बर............से कनेक्ट कर दीजिए!)

34. Send him/her up to my room.

Usé méré room mén bhéj dén.

(उसे मेरे रूम में भेज दें.)

35. Tell him/her to wait in the lobby.

Usé lobby mén intézār káráné ké liye káhen.

(उसे लॉबी में इन्तज़ार करने के लिये कहें.)

36. I'll be there within half an hour.

    Main wáhān ādhā ghánté mén páhuńch jāoongā.

    (मैं वहाँ आधा घन्टे में पहुंच जाऊंगा.)

37. I will return in the evening.

    Main shāmko lautoongā.

    (मैं शाम को लौटूंगा.)

38. Tell the visitor to come on Monday.

    Āgántuk ko somwār ko āné ké liye káhén'.

    (आगन्तुक को सोमवार को आने के लिये कहे.)

39. It is room number three ó four.

    Yeh room number teen sau chār hai.

    (यह रूम नम्बर तीन सौ चार है.)

40. Send me some warm water.

    Kripaya thódā gárám pānee bhijwā dijiye.

    (कृपया थोड़ा गरम पानी भिजवा दीजिये.)

41. By what time the lunch will be ready?

    Kitné bajé ták lunch taiyār ho jayegā?

    (कितने बजे तक लंच तैयार हो जाएगा?)

42. Uptil what time you are open for the dinner?

Rāt mén āp káb ták khānā serve karté hain?

(रात में आप कब तक खाना सर्व करते हैं?)

43. What is the dish of the day?

Āj kā 'the dish of the day' kyā hai?

(आज का द डिश ऑफ द डे क्या है?)

44. Kindly serve the meal in my room!

Kripáyā méré room mén khānā bhéj dén!

(कृपया मेरे रूम में खाना भेज दें!)

45. I am checking out.

Main hotel chhoḍ r'ahā hoon'.

(मैं होटेल छोड़ रहा हूँ.)

46. Call a taxi for me.

Méré liyé ék taxi bula dén.

(मेरे लिये एक टैक्सी बुला दें.)

47. Yes, straight to the Airport.

Hān, seedhé Airport ko.

(हां, सीधे एयरपोर्ट को.)

At a tourist place

1. Is there any office of Tourism department here?

   Kyā yáhān Tourism vibhāg kā koi office hai?

   (क्या यहाँ टूरिज्म विभाग का कोई ऑफिस है?)

2. Yes, I want a tourist guide.

   Hān, mujhé ék tourist guide chāhiyé.

   (हाँ, मुझे एक टूरिस्ट गाइड चाहिए.)

3. Are you a registered guide?

   Kyā āp ék registered guide hain?

   (क्या आप एक रजिस्टर्ड गाइड हैं?)

4. Kindly show me your I-card.

   Kripáyā mujhe ápnā I-card dikhāiyé.

   (कृपया मुझे अपना आई-कार्ड दिखाइये.)

5. How much time will it take to see this place

completely?

Yéh poori jágáh dekháné mén kitná wáktá
lágégā?

(यह पूरी जगह देखने में कितना वक्त लगेगा?)

6. I do not have seven days....will three days
   do?

   Méré pās sāt din ńáheen haiń......kyā teen din
   kāfee hongé?

   (मेरे पास सात दिन नहीं है.....क्या तीन दिन काफी
   होंगे?)

7. Do you charge your fee on daily basis?

   Kyā āp 'daily basis' pár apnā mehnátānā lété
   hain?

   (क्या आप 'डेली बेसिस' पर अपना मेहनताना लेते
   है?)

8. How much do you charge for your package
   of three days?

   Apné teen din ké package ké liyé āp kitna
   lete hain?

   (अपने तीन दिन के पैकेज के लिये आप कितना
   लेते हैं?)

9. Ok, get tickets for the three of us.

Theek hai, hám teen logon' ké liyé ticket le lijiye.

(ठीक है, हम तीन लोगों के लिये टिकट ले लीजिये.)

10. Do you know the history of this monumnet with details?

   Kyā āp is smārák kā itihās poori táráh sé jānáte hain?

   (क्या आप इस स्मारक का इतिहास पूरी तरह से जानते हैं?)

11. How old it is?

   Yeh kitnā purānā hai?

   (यह कितना पुराना है?)

12. Was the king assasinated?

   Kyā rājā ki rajneetik hátyā huee?

   (क्या राजा की राजनीतिक हत्या हुई?)

13. Did the queen die a natural death?

   Kyā rānee swābhāwik mrityu se máree?

   (क्या रानी स्वाभाविक मृत्यु से मरी?)

14. Did the prince rule after the king's death?

   Kyā rājā kee mrityu ké bād yuvárāj né shāsán kiya?

(क्या राजा की मृत्यु के बाद युवराज ने शासन किया?)

15. How many wives did he have?

    Uskee kitnee patniyān theen'?

    (उसकी कितनी पत्लियाँ थीं?)

16. Tell me the exact period of his rule.

    Uske shāsán kāl kee sáhee avádhi mujhe bátāén.

    (उसके शासन काल की सही अवधि मुझे बतायें.)

17. Did he have any brothers?

    Kyā uské koee bhāee bhee thé?

    (क्या उसके कोई भाई भी थे?)

18. Was he enthroned during his father's life time itself?

    Kyā uské pitā ké jeeván kāl mén hee usé rajgáddee mil gayee thee?

    (क्या उसके पिता के जीवन काल में ही उसे राजगद्दी मिल गई थी?)

19. Who was the actual heir?

    Aslee uttárādhikāree kaun thā?

    (असली उत्तराधिकारी कौन था?)

20. Why does this arch stand separately?

Yeh mehrāb alág-thálág kyon' hai?

(यह मेहराब अलग-थलग क्यों है?)

21. Let's now enter the main structure.

Āiyé, mukhyá hissé mén chalén.

(आइये, अब मुख्य हिस्से में चलें.)

22. Let's choose the right path.

Chaliyé hám dāhinā rāstā chunáté hain.

(चलिये हम दाहिना रास्ता चुनते हैं.)

23. Do we have to ascend any staircases?

Kyā hámén koee jeené chaḍháné hongé?

(क्या हमें कोई जीनें चढ़ने होंगे?)

24. Roughly how many steps?

Lágbhág kitneen' seeḍhiyān?

(लगभग कितनी सीढ़ियां?)

25. Is it a one way route?

Kyā yeh ek 'one way' rāstā hai?

(क्या यह एक 'वन वे' रास्ता है?)

26. Is the exit route rather tough?

Kyā bāhár nikálne kā rāstā zyādáh káṭhin hai?

(क्या बाहर निकलने का रास्ता ज्यादा कठिन है?)

27. **Where does it open?**

Yéh káhān khulátā hai?

(यह कहां खुलता है?)

28. Were any foreign engineers involved in this construction?

Kyā isé bánāné mén koee videshi engineer bhee lágé thé?

(क्या इसे बनाने में कोई विदेशी इन्जीनियर भी लगे थे?)

29. Can you read the inscription on this tomb?

Kyā tum is kábrá pár ki likhāwáṭ parh sákáté ho?

(क्या तुम इस कब्र पर की लिखावट पढ़ सकते हो?)

30. Tell me what it says?

Mujhé bátāo ki yeh kyā káhátee hai?

(मुझे बताओं कि यह क्या कहती हैं?)

31. Does this minarette signify some thing special?

Kyā is meenār kā koee khās máhátwá hai?

(क्या इस मीनार का कोई खास महत्व है?)

32. Is it necessary to ignite incense sticks here?

Kyā yáhān agárbáttiyān jáláná zárooree hai?

(क्या यहां अगरबत्तियां जलाना जरूरी है?)

33. Where does this tunnel lead to?

   Yeh suráng káhān jātee hai?

   (यह सुरंग कहाँ जाती है?)

34. Was it constructed later on?

   Kyā yéh bād mén bánāyee gáyee?

   (क्या यह बाद में बनायी गई?)

35. Was the king liked by the people?

   Kyā rājā ko jánātā pásánd kárátee thee?

   (क्या राजा को जनता पसन्द करती थी?)

36. Can I see through that ventilator?

   Kyā main us roshándān sé bāhár dékh sákátā hoon'?

   (क्या मैं उस रोशनदान से बाहर देख सकता हूँ?)

37. What do you call this structure in Hindi?

   Is ráchánā ko āp Hindi mén kyā káháte hain?

   (इस रचना को आप हिन्दी में क्या कहते हैं?)

38. And what is the name of this material?

   Aur is sāmágree kā kyā nām hai?

   (और इस सामग्री का क्या नाम है?)

39. Can one reach outside the dome?

Kyā koee gumbád ké bāháree hisse ták jā sakatā hai?

(क्या कोई गुम्बद के बाहरी हिस्से तक जा सकता है?)

40. Are these walls hollow?

Kyā yeh deewarén khokhálee hain?

(क्या यह दीवारें खोखली है?)

41. Are these really solid?

Kyā yéh sáchmuch ṭhosá hain?

(क्या ये सचमुच ठोस हैं?)

42. Were these made deliberately so?

Kyā yéh jān-boojh kár aisee bánāyee gáyee theen?

(क्या ये जान बूझकर ऐसी बनाई गई थीं?)

43. How much time it took to complete?

Isé poora honé mén kitnā waktá lágā thā?

(इसे पूरा होने में कितना वक्त लगा था?)

44. Were local artists and labourers employed?

Kyā 'local' kāreegáron aur majdooron ko lágāyā gáyā thā?

(क्या 'लोकल' कारीगरों और मजदूरों को लगाया

गया था?)

45. Who was the chief architect?

Mukhyá vāstukār kaun thā?

(मुख्य वास्तुकार कौन था?)

46. Whose statue is this?

Yéh kiskee murtee hai?

(यह किसकी मूर्ति है?)

47. Can I go into sanctum sanctorum of the
     temple?

*Kyā main mandir ke garbhá-grihá mén jā
sákátā hoon'?*

(क्या मैं मन्दिर के गर्भगृह में जा सकता हूँ?)

48. What material this is made of?

Yéh kis 'material' kā bánā hai?

(यह किस मैटीरियल का बना है?)

49. Which god does this temple belong to?

Yeh mándir kis devátā kā hai?

(यह मन्दिर किस देवता का है?)

50. Do we have to take our shoes off?

Kyā hámén apáné jooté utáráné hongé?

(क्या हमें अपने जूते उतारने होंगे?)

51. Is there some eating place here?

 Kyā yáhān koi khāné lāyák jágáh hai?

 (क्या यहां कोई खाने लायक जगह है?)

52. Is the prasad given to everyone?

 Kyā prásād sáb ko diyā jātā hai?

 (क्या प्रसाद सब को दिया जाता है?)

53. Is it palatable for a foreigner?

 Kyā ék vidéshi ké liyé yéh swādishtá hoga?

 (क्या एक विदेशी के लिये यह स्वादिष्ट होगा?)

54. And adequate in quantity too?

 Aur mātrā mén bhee kāfee?

 (और मात्रा में भी काफ़ी?)

55. How far is the beach?

 Yáhān sé sámudrá kā kinārā kitnee door hai?

 (यहां से समुद्र का किनारा कितनी दूर है?)

56. Does the managment accept any monetary contributious?

 Kyā management kisee táráh kā ārthik sáháyog sweekār kárátá hai?

 (क्या मैनेजमेन्ट किसी तरह का आर्थिक सहयोग स्वीकार करता है?)

57.   Then, where is this counter?

Táb, yéh counter káhān hai?

(तब यह काउन्टर कहाँ है?)

58.   Can we hire swimming costume here?

Kyā yáhān swimming costume kirāyé pár mil sákáte hain?

(क्या यहाँ स्विमिंग कॉस्ट्यूम किराये पर मिल सकते हैं?)

59.   Is there facility for sun bathing?

Kyā yahān dhoop sénkáné ki suwidhā hai?

(क्या यहां धूप सेंकने की सुविधा है?)

60.   Are only foreigners allowed?

Kyā sirf vidéshiyon ko hee anumáti hai?

(क्या सिर्फ विदेशियों को ही अनुमति है?)

61.   How does one reach that island?

Us ṭāpoo ták kaise jāyā jātā hai?

(उस टापू तक कैसे जाया जाता है?)

62.   By steamer, motor boat or ferry?

Steamer meń, motor boat sé yā ferrysé?

स्टीमर में, मोटर बोट से या फेरी से?

63.   Do you have any of your friends in Manali?

Kyā āpké koi dost MÁNĀLI mén bhee hain?

(क्या आपके कोई दोस्त मनाली में भी हैं?)

64. Yes, we want to visit that hilly area also.

Hān, hám woh páhāḍee 'area' bhee dekhánā chāháte hain.

(हाँ, हम वह पहाड़ी 'एरिया' भी देखना चाहते हैं.)

65. Thank you very much for your excellent job.

Apke shāndār kām ké liyé bahut-hahut dhanyáwād.

(आपके शानदार काम के लिये बहुत-बहुत धन्यवाद!)

66. Here is your fee......keep the change.

Yéh āpákee fees hai—'change' rákh lijiye.

(यह आपकी फीस है—चेन्ज रख लीजिये.)

General Sentences for Every Day Use

1. Hello, how are you?
   Hello, āp kaise haiń?
   हेलो आप कैसे हैं?

2. I am fine.
   Main achhā hoon'.
   मैं अच्छा हूँ.

3. Bring me coffee.
   Méré liyé coffee lāiyé.
   मेरे लिये कॉफी लाइये.

4. Stay there.
   Waheen ṭháháriyé.
   वहीं ठहरिये.

5. Come here.
   Yahān āiyé.

यहां आइये.

6. Go inside.

Andár jāiyé.

अन्दर जाइये.

7. Wait in the lawn.

Lāwn mén intezār kijiyé.

लॉन में इन्तज़ार कीजिये.

8. Meet at the gate.

Gate pár miliyé.

गेट पर मिलिये.

9. Walk on the pavemnet.

'Footpath' pár chaliyé.

फुटपाथ पर चलिये.

10. It is not a parking place.

Yeh parking kee jágáh naheen hai.

यह पार्किंग की जगह नहीं है.

11. The pen is in the box.

Kálám box mén hai.

कलम बॉक्स में है.

12. Your shoe is under the table.

Āpkā joota table ké neeché hai.

आपका जूता टेबल के नीचे है.

13. The green stripe is below the white one.

Háree patti safed patti ké neeché hai.

हरी पट्टी सफेद पट्टी के नीचे है.

14. Lift the ball from the ground.

Zámeen pár sé génd uthā lijiye.

ज़मीन पर से गेंद उठा लीजिये.

15. Take it.

Yeh lijiyé.

यह लीजिये.

16. Give me the paper.

Mujhe kāgáz dijiyé.

मुझे कागज़ दीजिये.

17. It is cold outside.

Bāhár thandak hai.

बाहर ठन्डक है.

18. It is rather humid inside.

Andár námee zyādáh hai.

अन्दर नमी ज्यादा है.

19. It still appears dirty.

Yeh abhee bhee gándā lág ráhā hai.

यह अभी भी गन्दा लग रहा है.

20. She has not come yet.

Woh abhee ták naheen āyee hai.

वह अभी तक नहीं आयी है।

21. Yes, now it appears clean.

Hān, áb yéh sāf déekh ráhā hai.

हां अब यह साफ दीख रहा है।

22. Go upstairs.

Upár jāo.

ऊपर जाओ।

23. Come downstairs

Neeché āo.

नीचे आओ।

24. I Want a washer man.

Mujhé ék dhobi chāhiye.

मुझे एक धोबी चाहिए।

25. Is there a laundary nearby?

Kyā nazdeek méń koi laundary hai?

क्या नज़दीक में कोई लॉन्ड्री है?

26. Can she iron this shirt well?

Kyā woh yéh shirt theek sé iron kár sakatee hai?

क्या वह यह शर्ट ठीक से आयरन कर सकती है?

27. Call her quickly.

Usé jáldee bulāo.

उसे जल्दी बुलाओ.

28. It is getting late.

Dér ho ráhee hai.

देर हो रही है.

29. It is quite early.

abheè kafee jáldee hai.

अभी काफी जल्दी है.

30. Run faster.

Aur téz dauḍo.

और तेज़ दौड़ो.

31. Walk slowly.

Dheeré chálo.

धीरे चलो.

32. The newpaper is on the bed.

Akhbār bistár pár hai.

अखबार बिस्तर पर है.

33. The dictionary is above the magazine.

Dictionary magazine ké oopár hai.

डिक्शनरी मैगजीन के ऊपर है.

34. The post office is in front.

Post office sāmáne hai.

पोस्ट आफिस सामने है।

35. What lies behind it?

Iské peechhé kyā hai?

इसके पीछे क्या है?

36. There is a banyan tree beside the mosque.

Masjid kee bágál mén ék bárgád kā péḍ hai.

मस्जिद की बगल में, एक बरगद का पेड़ है।

37. Are you from Oriental Travels?

Kyā āp oriental Travels sé hain'?

क्या आप ओरियन्टल ट्रैवेल्स से हैं?

38. Will this telephonic talk do?

Kyā is telephonic bāt sé kām chál jāyegā?

क्या इस टेलीफोनिक बात से काम चल जाएगा?

39. We want to visit Nainital.

Hám Nainital jānā chāháte hain.

हम नैनीताल जाना चाहते हैं?

40. Do you provide any package tours?

Kyā āp koee 'package tour' kárāte hain?

क्या आप कोई पैकेज टूर कराते हैं?

41. For four adults.

Chār bāligon' ke liye.

चार बालिगों के लिये.

42. No, there are no children.

Naheen, yáhān koee báchché náheen hain.

नहीं, यहां कोई बच्चे नहीं हैं.

43. Yes, no one is under twenty five.

Hān, páchchees ké neeché koee náheen hai.

हां, पच्चीस के नीचे कोई नहीं है.

44. For four days including up and down journey?

Āne aur jāné sáhit chār din?

आने और जाने सहित चार दिन?

45. Including all the meals?

Sabhee bhojánon' ke sāth?

सभी भोजनों के साथ?

46. Exculding lunches?

Din ke khānon' ko chhoḍ kar?

दिन के खानों को छोड़ कर?

47. You are asking for too much.

Āp zyādáh māng rahe hain.

आप ज्यादा मांग रहे हैं.

48. No, it's not reasonable.

Naheen, yéh uchit naheen hai.

नहीं, यह उचित नहीं है.

49. Which vehicle will you provide?

Āp kaun see gāḍee hamén déngé?

आप कौन-सी गाड़ी हमें देंग?

50. Yes, an A.C.Qualis will be better.

Hān, ek air conditioned Qualis theek ráhégee.

हां, एक एयर कन्डीशन्ड क्वालिस ठीक रहेगी.

51. Is it a public telephone booth?

Kyā yéh ék public telephone booth hai?

क्या यह एक पब्लिक टेलीफोन बूथ है?

52. Can I make an ISD call from here?

Kyā main ek ISD call yáhān sé kár sákátā hoon'?

क्या मैं एक आई.एस.डी. कॉल यहाँ से कर सकता हूँ?

53. And local calls as well?

Aur local call bhee?

और लोकल कॉल भी?

54. Do you have internet facility also?

Kyā āpke pās internet facility bhee hai?

क्या आपके पास इन्टरनेट फेसिलिटी भी है?

55. Can I check my E-mail here?

Kyā main apnā E-mail yáhān dékátā hoon?

क्या मैं अपना ई-मेल यहाँ देख सकता हूँ?

56.   At What rate you charge for net surfing?

Netsurfing ke liyé āp kis dár sé charge karate hain?

नेट सर्फिंग के लिये आप किस दर से चार्ज करते हैं?

57.   So you sell antiques...?

Achhā to āp antique bén'cháté hain?

अच्छा, तो आप एन्टीक बेंचते हैं?

58.   And modern art works?

Aur adhunik kálākritiyān?

और आधुनिक कलाकृतियां...?

59.   How much is that silken cap?

Us reshámee topee ki kitánee keemát hai?

उस रेशमी टोपी की कितनी· कीमत है?

60.   No, the red one behind the orange one.

Naheen, nārángee wali ké peechhé lāl wālee.

नहीं, नारंगी वाली के पीछे लाल वाली.

61.   My god, is it so expensive?

My god, yeh itnā máhéngā hai?

माई गॉड, यह इतना महंगा है?

62. Some thing cheaper?

   Koee sástee cheez?

   कोई सस्ती चीज़?

63. Does this bronze piece qualify as an antique?

   Kyā bronze ka yéh piece antique kee ginátee mén ātā hai?

   क्या ब्रौन्ज का यह पीस एन्टीक की गिनती में आता है?

64. O.K., pack it.

   Theek hai, isé pack kár dén.

   ठीक है, इसे पैक कर दें.

65. Don't delay.

   Dér mát kijiye.

   देर मत कीजिये.

66. Tell him to keep his fingers off the piece.

   Usko káhiyé ki woh apnee ungliyān us piece se door rakhé.

   उसको कहिये कि वह अपनी उंगलियां उस पीस से दूर रखे.

67. My shoes need polish.

   Méré jooton' ko polish kee zároorát hai.

मेरे जूतों को पौलिश की ज़रूरत है.

68. I need a hair cut.

Mujhé bāl kátwānén' hain'.

मुझे बाल कटवाने हैं.

69. Will I have to go to saloon?

Kyā mujhé saloon ták jānā hogā?

क्या मुझे सैलून तक जाना होगा?

70. What do you mean?

Tumhārā kyā mátláb hai?

तुम्हारा क्या मतलब है?

71. Why are you worried?

Tum chintit kyon' ho?

तुम चिन्तित क्यों हो?

72. How do you cook it?

Āp isé kaisé pákāte hain?

आप इसे कैसे पकाते हैं?

73. Where did you get it?

Yéh tumhén káhān' milā?

यह तुम्हें कहाँ मिला?

74. Which of these is yours?

Inmén sé káun sā tumhārā hai?

इनमें से कौन-सा तुम्हारा है?

75. When do we go?

Hám káb jāyéngé?

हम कब जायेंगे?

76. Sharpen this pencil.

Is pencil ko nukeelā káro.

इस पेंसिल को नुकीला करो.

77. What is the matter?

Kyā bāt hai?

क्या बात है?

78. It does not sound good.

Yéh achhā náheen lágátā.

यह अच्छा नहीं लगता.

79. I am ready for last two hours.

Main pichhlé do ghánton' sé taiyār hoon'.

मैं पिछले दो घन्टों से तैयार हूँ.

80. I don't believe it.

Main iska vishwās naheen kárátā.

मैं इसका विश्वास नहीं करता.

Hindi Vocabulary

1	ant	चींटी	chinti
2	a	एक	ek
3	aback	पीछे	piche
4	ability	योग्यता	yogyta
5	above	के ऊपर	ke upar
6	abroad	विदेश में	videsh main
7	absorb	सोख लेना	sokh lena
8	accept	स्वीकार करना	swikar karna
9	accuracy	ठीक-ठाक	theek-thak

10	accuse	दोष लगाना	dosh lagana
11	acerbate	चिढ़ाना	chidhana
12	ache	दर्द	dard
13	acne	मुँहासा	muhansha
14	acrimonious	उग्र	ugra
15	acrobat	कलाबाज़	kalabaj
16	actual	वास्तविक	wastwik
17	acute	नुकीला	nukeela
18	adage	कहावत	kahawat
19	adept	निपुण	nipun
20	adhere	चिपकना	chipkana
21	adjective	विशेषण	visheshan
22	advise	सलाह	salah
23	afternoon	दोपहर	dopahar
24	aid	सहायता	sahcyata

127

25	alarm	चेतावनी	chetawanee
26	alight	उतरना	utarna
27	all	सब	sab
28	allay	शान्त करना	shant karna
29	allot	बाँटना	bantna
30	almost	प्राय:	prayah
31	aloud	जोर से	jor se
32	already	अभी तक	abhee tak
33	also	भी	bhee
34	alter	बदल देना	badal dena
35	although	यद्यपि	yadyapi
36	always	सदा	sada
37	amass	जमा करना	jama karna
38	amative	प्रेमी	premee
39	amaze	चकित	chakit

128

40	amazon	वीरांगना	*veerangana*
41	ambo	मंच	*manch*
42	ample	विस्तृत	*vistrit*
43	and	और	*aur*
44	Anno Domini	इस्वी सन्	*ishwee san*
45	announcement	सूचना	*soochana*
46	annoy	चिढ़ाना	*chidhana*
47	annual	वार्षिक	*warshik*
48	answer	जवाब	*jawab*
49	aporia	संदेह	*sandeh*
50	appear	दिखाई देना	*dikhaee dena*
51	approach	पहुँच	*pahunch*
52	April	अप्रेल	*aprail*
53	area	क्षेत्र	*kshetra*
54	arm	हाथ	*haanth*

129

55	arow	पंक्तिबद्ध	panktibaddh
56	arride	संतोष देना	santosh dena
57	arrive	पहुँचना	pahunchana
58	arrow	तीर	teer
59	art	कला	kala
60	artist	कलाकार	kalakar
61	ask	पूछना	poochhana
62	attend	उपस्थित	upasthit
63	augment	बढ़ाना	badhana
64	August	अगस्त	agast
65	aunt	चाची	chachee
66	auto	स्वतः	swatah
67	autumn	शरद	sharad
68	avoid	से दूर रहना	se door rahana
69	axe	कुल्हाड़ा	kulhara

130

70	baby	बच्चा	bachcha
71	bachelor	कुमार	kumar
72	background	पृष्ठभूमि	prishthbhumi
73	backside	नितम्ब	nitamb
74	bad	बुरा	bura
75	badinage	परिहास	parihas
76	bag	थैला	thaila
77	bake	पकाना	pakana
78	balancing	संतुलन	santulan
79	ball	गेंद	gend
80	bamboo	बाँस	bans
81	banana	केला	kela
82	bangle	चूड़ी	churee
83	bank	बैंक	baink
84	barb	काँटा	kanta

85	barber	नाई	naee
86	barren	बंजर	banjar
87	bathroom	स्नान-घर	snan-ghar
88	bay	खाड़ी	kharee
89	beast	चौपाया	chaupaya
90	beautiful	सुन्दर	sundar
91	because	लेकिन	lekin
92	beck	इशारा	ishara
93	bedroom	शयनकक्ष	shayankaksh
94	beef	गोमांस	gomans
95	befool	धोखा देना	dhokha dena
96	before	पहले	pahle
97	begin	आरम्भ करना	aarambh karna
98	behalf	की ओर से	kee or se
99	belief	विश्वास	vishwas

132

100	believe	विश्वास करना	vishwas karna
101	belle	सुन्दरी	sundari
102	better	बेहतर	behatar
103	between	बीच में	beech main
104	beyond	बाहर	bahar
105	Bible	बाइबिल	baibil
106	bilk	ठगना	thagna
107	bill	बिल	bil
108	bind	बाँधना	bandhna
109	bird	पक्षी	pakshee
110	bitch	कुतिया	kutiya
111	bizarre	अनोखा	anokha
112	black	काला	kala
113	blackboard	श्यामपट्ट	shyampat
114	blast	धमाका	dhamaka

115	blear	धुंधला	dhundhla
116	bless	आशीर्वाद देना	aashirwad dena
117	blood	खून	khoon
118	blue	नीला	neela
119	body	शरीर	sharir
120	bone	हड्डी	haddee
121	book	किताब	kitab
122	border	किनारा	kinara
123	boss	स्वामी	swamee
124	bottle	बोतल	botal
125	boy	लड़का	larka
126	bread	चपाती	chapati
127	breakfast	नास्ता	nasta
128	breast	वक्षस्थल	vakshsthal
129	broad	चौड़ा	chaura

130	broom	झाड़ू	jharoo
131	brother	भाई	bhai
132	bucket	बाल्टी	balti
133	build	बनाना	banana
134	but	लेकिन	lekin
135	buy	खरीदना	kharidna
136	cabbage	बंदगोभी	bandgobi
137	call	बुलाना	bulana
138	capital	राजधानी	rajdhanee
139	cardamom	इलायची	elaichi
140	careful	सावधान	sawdhan
141	carrot	गाजर	gajar
142	carry	ढोना	dhona
143	case	मुकदमा	mukadma
144	cash	रोकड़	rokar

145	cauliflower	फुलगोभी	phul gobi
146	chair	कुर्सी	kursi
147	charm	सौजन्य	saujanya
148	chat	बातचीत	batcheet
149	cheap	सस्ता	sasta
150	cheese	पनीर	paneer
151	cheque	चेक	chek
152·	chick peas	चना	chana
153	child	बच्चा	bachcha
154	choice	चुनाव	chunav
155	church	गिरजाघर	girjaghar
156	cigar	सिगार	sigar
157	cinema	सिनेमा	sinema
158	Cinnamon	दालचीनी	dalcheenee
159	city	शहर	shahar

160	class	कक्षा	kaksha
161	classical	शास्त्रीय	shastreeya
162	clay oven	तंदूर	tandoor
163	climate	जलवायु	jalwayu
164	close	बंद	band
165	cloth	कपड़ा	kapra
166	cloud	बादल	badal
167	coal	कोयला	koyala
168	coast	तट	tat
169	cock	मुर्गा	murga
170	coconut	नारियल	nariyal
171	coffee	कॉफी	kanfee
172	cold	ठंडा	thanda
173	colony	मण्डल	mandal
174	colour	रंग	rang

175	come	आना	aana
176	comedy	प्रहसन	prahasan
177	command	अधिकार	aadhikar
178	commerce	वाणिज्य	vanijya
179	committee	समिति	samiti
180	common	सामान्य	samanya
181	convert	बदलना	badlana
182	cool	शीतल	sheetal
183	copper	ताँबा	tamba
184	copy	प्रतिलिपि	pratilipi
185	cordial	हार्दिक	hardik
186	corn	मक्का	makka
187	correct	सटीक	sateek
188	cost	लागत	lagat
189	cotton	कपास	kapas

138

190	count	गिन्ना	ginana
191	country	देश	desh
192	courteous	शिष्ट	shisht
193	cousin	रिश्तेदार	rishtedar
194	cow	गाय	gay
195	crazy	पागल	pagal
196	cream	मलाई	malai
197	cucumber	ककड़ी	kakari
198	cup	कप	kap
199	currency	मुद्रा	mudra
200	curse	शाप	shap
201	damage	क्षति	kshti
202	dance	नाच	naach
203	darling	परमप्रिय	parampriya
204	data	आँकड़े	aankare

139

205	dating	तिथि-निर्धारण	tithi-nirdharan
206	daughter	बेटी	beti
207	day	दिन	din
208	dean	अध्यक्ष	adhyaksh
209	dear	प्रिय	priya
210	December	दिसम्बर	dismbar
211	decision	निर्णय	nirnay
212	delete	मिटाना	mitana
213	delicacy	कोमलता	komalata
214	describe	वर्णन करना	warnan
215	desire	चाहना	chahna
216	detain	रोकना	rokna
217	devil	शैतान	shaitan
218	dictionary	शब्दकोष	shabdkosh
219	difference	अन्तर	antar

140

220	difficult	कठिन	kathin
221	dike	बाँध	bandh
222	dim	मन्द	mand
223	dining room	भोजन-कक्ष	bhojan kaksha
224	distinguish	पहचानना	pahchanana
225	dither	थरथराहट	tharthrahat
226	dive	गोता	gota
227	doctor	चिकित्सक	chikitsak
228	dog	कुत्ता	kutta
229	dollar	डॉलर	dollar
230	door	दरवाजा	darwaza
231	doubt	सन्देह	sandeh
232	drama	नाटक	natak
233	drastic	प्रबल	prawal
234	dress	पोशाक	poshak

141

235	drink	पेय	*pey*
236	duplicate	दोहरा	*dohara*
237	dust	धूल	*dhool*
238	each	प्रत्येक	*pratyek*
239	ear	कान	*kan*
240	early	प्रातः कालीन	*pratah kalin*
241	ease	आराम	*aaram*
242	easy	आसान	*aasan*
243	eat	खाना	*khana*
244	Egg	अंडा	*Andaa*
245	eight	आठ	*aath*
246	eject	निकाल फेंकना	*nikal fenkana*
247	elbow	कोहनी	*kohni*
248	eleven	ग्यारह	*gyarah*
249	employ	प्रयोग करना	*prayog karna*

142

250	end	समाप्त	samapt
251	England	इंग्लैंड	england
252	English	अंग्रेजी	angreji
253	enjoy	उपभोग लेना	upbhog lena
254	enormous	विशाल	vishal
255	enough	काफी	kafe
256	enter	घुसना	ghusna
257	entire	सम्पूर्ण	sampurn
258	Europe	यूरोप	Europe
259	every day	प्रत्येक दिन	pratyek din
260	examination	परीक्षा	paricha
261	example	उदाहरण	udaharan
262	excuse	क्षमायाचना	kshmayachna
263	exercise	व्यायाम करना	wyayam karna
264	explain	समझाना	samjhana

143

265	expose	विवरण	vivran
266	extol	गुणगान करना	gungan karna
267	eye	आँख	ankh
268	face	चेहरा	chehra
269	factory	कम्पनी	company
270	fairy	परी	pari
271	fall	पतन	patan
272	family	परिवार	pariwar
273	famous	प्रसिद्ध	prasidh
274	far	दूर	door
275	fare	किराया	kiraya
276	farmer	किसान	kishan
277	fast	तेज	tez
278	fat	मोटा	mota
279	father	पिता	pita

144

280	favour	अनुग्रह	anugrah
281	feast	पर्व	paraw
282	feat	साहसिक कार्य	sahsik karya
283	February	फरवरी	ferwary
284	feces	मल	mal
285	feel	स्पर्श करना	saprash karna
286	fennel	काला जीरा	kala jira
287	festival	त्यौहार	tayohar
288	few	कुछ	kuch
289	field	मैदान	maidan
290	fifteen	पंद्रह	pandrah
291	fig	अंजीर	anjir
292	finalize	पूर्ण करना	purn karna
293	find	पाना	pana
294	finger	अंगुली	ungooli

295	fire	आग	aag
296	first	पहला	pehla
297	fish	मछली	machli
298	five	पाँच	panch
299	floor	फर्श	farsh
300	flounder	छटपटाना	chatpatana
301	flower	फूल	phool
302	foot	पैर	pair
303	for	के लिए	ke liye
304	foreign	विदेश	videsh
305	forest	जंगल	jungle
306	forget	भूल जाना	bhool jana
307	fort	किला	qila
308	forty	चालीस	chalis
309	forward	आगे	aage

146

		विकसित करना	viksit karna
310	Foster		
311	four	चार	chaar
312	France	फ्रांस	france
313	Friday	शुक्रवार	sukrawar
314	friend	दोस्त	dost
315	from	से	se
316	fruit	फल	phal
317	full	पूर्ण	poorn
318	gain	लाभ	labh
319	gap	छेद	ched
320	garden	बगीचा	bagicha
321	garment	कपड़ा	kapra
322	German	जर्मन	german
323	get	पाना	pana
324	get up	उठना	uthna

147

325	Ginger	अदरक	adrak
326	girl	लड़की	larki
327	give	देना	dena
328	glass	शीशा	seesa
329	glimmer	टिमटिमाना	timtimana
330	gloria	महिमा	mahima
331	glove	दस्ताना	dastana
332	go	जाना	jana
333	goat	बकरी	bakri
334	goddy	भावुक	bhawuk
335	godown	गोदाम	godam
336	gold	सोना	sona
337	golden	सुनहरा	sunahara
338	good	अच्छा	achcha
339	good-bye	विदाई	vidae

148

340	grammar	व्याकरण	wyakaran
341	grand	प्रधान	pradhan
342	grape	अंगुर	angur
343	green	हरा	hara
344	grim	निर्दय	nirday
345	groundnut	मुगफली	mung phali
346	guidon	ध्वज	dhawaz
347	hair	बाल	bal
348	half	आधा	aadha
349	halloo	ललकारना	lalkarna
350	halt	विराम	viram
351	hammer	हथौड़ा	hathora
352	hand	हाथ	hath
353	happy	सुखी	sukhee
354	hard	कड़ा	karah

149

355	harry	लूटना	lootna
356	haste	जल्दी	jaldi
357	hat	टोपी	topi
358	hate	बैर	bair
359	hauteur	अभिमान	abhiman
360	have	पास होना	pass hona
361	he	वह	wah
362	head	सिर	sir
363	health	स्वास्थ्य	swasthaya
364	heap	अम्बार	ambar
365	hear	सुनना	sunnaa
366	heart	दिल	dil
367	heat	ताप	tap
368	helicopter	हेलीकॉप्टर	helicopter
369	hen	मुर्गी	murgee

150

370	henna	मेंहदी	mehandi
371	here	यहाँ	yahan
372	high	ऊँचा	uncha
373	hire	किराया	kiraya
374	history	इतिहास	itihass
375	hope	आशा	aasa
376	horns	सींग	sing
377	horse	घोड़ा	ghora
378	hot	गर्म	garam
379	hotel	होटल	hotel
380	hour	घंटा	ghanta
381	house	घर	ghar
382	hoyden	चुलबुली लड़की	chulbuli ladki
383	hug	आलिंगन करना	aalingan karna
384	hundred	सौ	sao

151

385	hunger	भूख	bhukh
386	husband	पति	pati
387	I	मैं	main
388	identify	पहचान	pahchan
389	if	यदि	yadi
390	ignore	उपेक्षा करना	upechapi karna
391	impend	लटकना	latakna
392	important	महत्वपूर्ण	mahatwapurn
393	impossible	असंभव	asambhav
394	in	अंदर	andar
395	infinite	अनन्त	anant
396	inflect	मोड़ना	morna
397	ingulf	निगलना	nigalna
398	inhale	सांस खींचना	sans khichna
399	injure	चोट	chot

152

400	ink	स्याही	syahi
401	intelligent	बुद्धिमान	budhiman
402	intension	निश्चय	nischay
403	interest	अधिकार	adhikar
404	interfere	दखल करना	dakhal karna
405	January	जनवरी	janwary
406	join	मिलना	milna
407	joke	मजाक	majak
408	jolly	लोहा	loha
409	juice	रस	rus
410	July	जुलाई	july
411	June	जून	june
412	kindness	कृपा	kripa
413	king	राजा	raja
414	kiss	चुम्बन	chumban

153

415	kitchen	रसोईघर	rasoighar
416	knack	कौशल	kaushal
417	knap	तोड़ना	torna
418	knife	चाकु	chaku
419	knock	प्रहार	prahar
420	know	जानना	janana
421	kyrie	दया-याचना	daya-yachna
422	lane	गली	gali
423	language	भाषा	bhasha
424	large	बड़ा	bara
425	last	अन्त	aant
426	lasting	स्थायी	asthai
427	later	बाद में	baad main
428	lather	झाग	jhag
429	latria	आराधना	aaradhana

154

430	laugh	हँसना	hasna
431	lawyer	वकील	waquil
432	lazy	आलसी	aalsee
433	lead	सीसा	seesa
434	leaf	पत्ता	pata
435	learn	पढ़ना	padhana
436	leg	पैर	pair
437	Lemon	नींबु	nimbu
438	lento	धीरे-धीरे	dheere-dheere
439	less	कम	kum
440	lesson	पाठ	path
441	letter	पत्र	patra
442	library	पुस्तकालय	pustakalay
443	life	जीवन	jivan
444	light	हलका	halka

445	line	रेखा	rekha
446	link	कड़ी	karee
447	list	तालिका	talika
448	listen	सुनना	sunana
449	literary	साक्षरता	saksharta
450	literature	साहित्य	sahitya
451	little	छोटा	chota
452	live	निवास करना	niwas karna
453	liver	कलेजा	kaleza
454	lizard	छिपकली	chipkali
455	local	स्थानीय	asthaniye
456	locate	ठहराना	thahrana
457	long	लम्बा	lamba
458	lose	खो देना	kho dena
459	lost	नष्ट	nast

156

460	love	प्यार	*pyaar*
461	loving	स्नेही	*asnehi*
462	low	नीचे	*niche*
463	madonna	पागलपन	*pagalpan*
464	make	बनाना	*banana*
465	man	आदमी	*aadmi*
466	mango	आम	*aam*
467	manner	छंग	*chung*
468	map	नकशा	*naksha*
469	March	मार्च	*march*
470	Marsh	कच्छ	*kach*
471	May	मई	*may*
472	meal	भोजन	*bhojan*
473	meaning	अर्थ	*arth*
474	measure	माप	*maap*

157

475	meat	मांस	maans
476	member	सदस्य	sadasya
477	memorable	स्मरणीय	asmarniye
478	memory	स्मृति	asmriti
479	mental	मानसिक	mansik
480	mention	उल्लेख	ullekh
481	mercy	दया	daya
482	merry	आनन्दित	aanandit
483	micro	सूक्ष्म	sukshm
484	middle	मध्य	madhya
485	might	बल	bal
486	mile	मील	meel
487	milk	दूध	dudha
488	mine	सुरंग	surang
489	mineral	खनिज	khaniz

158

490	mint	पुदीना	pudina
491	minute	मिनट	minut
492	miss	चूकना	chukna
493	mistake	भूल	bhool
494	misuse	दुरुपयोग	curoopayog
495	modern	आधुनिक	aadhunik
496	Monday	सोमवार	somwar
497	money	पैसा	paisa
498	monkey	बंदर	bandar
499	month	महीना	maheena
500	moon	चाँद	chand
501	more	अधिक	adhik
502	morning	सुबह	subah
503	mosquito	मच्छर	machar
504	mother	माँ	ma

159

505	motivate	प्रेरित करना	prerit karna
506	mould	साँचा	sancha
507	mountain	पर्वत	parwat
508	mouth	मुँह	muh
509	movies	चलचित्र	chalchitra
510	Mr.	श्रीमान्	shriman
511	Mrs.	श्रीमति	shrimati
512	much	बहुत	bahut
513	mud	कीचड़	kichar
514	mushroom	मशरूम	mashroom
515	music	संगीत	sangeet
516	my	मेरा	mera
517	name	नाम	naam
518	narrow	संकीर्ण	sankirn
519	native	जन्मजात	janamjat

520	natural	स्वभाविक	swabhawik
521	near	नजदीक	nazdeek
522	nearby	निकट	nikat
523	need	आवश्यकता	aawasyakta
524	needle	सूई	sui
525	nerve	नस	nas
526	new	नया	naya
527	newspaper	अखबार	akhbar
528	next	अगला	agla
529	nib	दबाना	dabana
530	night	रात	raat
531	nine	नौ	nau
532	nipple	स्तनाग्र	astanagra
533	noble	महान	mahan
534	nobody	कोई नहीं	koi nahin

161

535	nod	सिर हिलाना	sir hilana
536	north	उत्तर	uttar
537	nose	नाक	nak
538	nothing	कुछ नहीं	kuch nahin
539	notice	सूचना	suchna
540	novel	उपन्यास	upanyas
541	November	नवम्बर	nawamber
542	now	अब	ab
543	observe	पालन करना	pagal karna
544	October	अक्टूबर	aqtober
545	octuple	अठगुना	aathguna
546	offer	अर्पण	aarpan
547	office	कार्यालय	karyalaya
548	officialese	दफ्तरी भाषा	daftari bhasa
549	often	अकसर	aksar

550	oil	तेल	tel
551	old	पुराना	purana
552	olid	बदबूदार	badbudara
553	omit	छोड़ देना	chor dena
554	on	ऊपर	oopar
555	once	एक बार	ek bar
556	one	एक	ek
557	onion	प्याज	piaz
558	only	केवल	kewal
559	open	खुला	khula
560	operate	परिचालन करना	parichalam karna
561	opportunity	अवसर	aawsar
562	or	अथवा	aathwa
563	orange	नारंगी	narangee

163

564	ordinary	मामूली	mamulee
565	ought	कुछ भी	kuch bhee
566	out	बाहर	bahar
567	outgoing	निर्गमि	nirgamee
568	phase	अवस्था	awastha
569	pain	दर्द	dard
570	paint	रंग भरना	rang bharna
571	palace	राजभवन	rajbhawan
572	palm	हथेली	hatheli
573	paper	कागज	kagaj
574	part	हिस्सा	hissa
575	party	दल	dal
576	pass	उत्तीर्ण होना	uthirn hona
577	passion	मनोभाव	manobhaw
578	path	रास्ता	rasta

164

579	pause	विराम	viram
580	pay	वेतन	wetan
581	peas	मटर	Mattar
582	pen	कलम	kalam
583	people	लोग	log
584	perfect	सम्पूर्ण	sampurn
585	person	व्यक्ति	wyakti
586	perspire	पसीना बहाना	pasina bahana
587	payee	पानेवाला	panewala
588	physical	शारीरिक	sareerik
589	picked	चुनिन्दा	chuninda
590	pickle	अचार	achar
591	picture	चित्र	chitra
592	pilot	चालक	chalak
593	place	स्थान	asthan

594	plain	मैदान	*maidan*
595	play	खेल	*khel*
596	please	कृपया	*kripaya*
597	plosive	स्पर्श	*asparsh*
598	poet	कवि	*kavi*
599	poetic	कवि का	*kavi ka*
600	poetry	काव्य	*kavya*
60r	point	बिन्दु	*vindu*
602	pompous	शानदार	*sandar*
603	poor	गरीब	*garib*
604	possible	सम्भव	*sambaw*
605	post office	डाकघर	*dakghar*
606	potato	आलू	*aaloo*
607	practice	व्यवहार	*wayawhar*
608	prefer	चाहना	*chahna*

166

609	preparation	तैयारी	tayaree
610	prepare	तैयार करना	tayar karna
611	pretty	सुन्दर	sundar
612	principal	प्रधानाचार्य	pradhancharya
613	probable	संभावित	sambhawit
614	produce	तैयार करना	taiyar karna
615	professor	आचार्य	aacharya
616	progress	प्रगति	pragati
617	pronounce	सुनाना	sunana
618	pronunciation	उच्चारण	ucharan
619	public	सार्वजनिक	sarwajanik
620	publicity	प्रचार	prachar
621	publish	प्रकाशन	prakashan
622	pull	खींचना	khichana
623	pulsate	धड़कना	dharakna

167

624	qualification	योग्यता	yogyata
625	quality	विशेषता	visesta
626	quarter	चौथाई	chouthai
627	queen	रानी	rani
628	question	प्रश्न	prashna
629	quit	मुक्त	mukt
630	quoad	के विषय में	ke visay main
631	quote	भाव बताना	bhaw batana
632	rage	रोष	rosh
633	rejoice	खुश करना	khush karna
634	relax	ढीला करना	dhila karna
635	remark	देखना	dekhna
636	remember	याद करना	yaad karna
637	renew	नया	naya
638	repeat	दोहराना	doharana

168

639	replete	भरापूरा	bharapura
640	request	निवेदन	niwedan
641	resist	विरोध करना	virodh karna
642	resource	साधन	sadhan
643	respire	सांस लेना	sans lena
644	rest	आराम करना	aaram karna
645	result	परिणाम	parinam
646	return	लौटना	lautna
647	reverse	उलटा	ulta
648	review	पुनरीक्षण	punareekshan
649	rice	चावल	chawal
650	rich	अमीर	aamir
651	right	सही	sahi
652	right-down	पक्का	pakka
653	ring	अंगूठी	anguthi

654	river	नदी	nadi
655	road	सड़क	sadak
656	rogue	दुर्जन	durjan
657	romance	रोमांस	romance
658	room	कमरा	kamra
659	rope	रस्सी	rasee
660	round	गोल	goal
661	Royal	शाही	shahi
662	rule	नियम	niyam
663	ruler	शासक	sasak
664	run	दौड़	daur
665	sad	उदास	udas
666	Saffron	केसर	kesar
667	salt	नमक	namak
668	same	एक ही	ekhi

669	sand	रेत	rait
670	Saturday	शनिवार	saniwar
671	say	बोलना	bolna
672	school	विद्यालय	vidyalay
673	scold	डाँटना	datna
674	second	दूसरा	dushra
675	secret	गुप्त	gupt
676	see	देखना	dekhna
677	seek	खोजना	khojna
678	sell	बेचना	bechna
679	sentence	वाक्य	waqya
680	September	सितम्बर	sitamber
681	serve	सेवा करना	sewa karna
682	server	सेवक	sewak
683	servile	चापलूसी	chaploosee

171

684	seven	सात	saat
685	several	अनेक	anek
686	sewing	सिलाई	silaee
687	sex	लिंग	ling
688	shade	छाया	chaya
689	shanty	कुटिया	kutiya
690	shave	हजामत	hazamat
691	she	वह	wah
692	shirt	कमीज	kameez
693	shoe	जूता	joota
694	shop	दुकान	dukan
695	shore	तट	tat
696	short	छोटा	chota
697	show	दिखाना	dikhana
698	sick	झपटना	jhaptana

172

699	sight	दृश्य	drishya
700	signature	हस्ताक्षर	hastakshar
701	silent	मौन	maun
702	silk	रेशम	resham
703	silver	चाँदी	chandee
704	similar	मिलता–जुलता	milta-julta
705	simple	सरल	saral
706	sing	गाना	gana
707	sit down	बैठ जाना	baith jana
708	six	छः	chah
709	size	आकार	aakar
710	skin	चमड़ा	chamra
711	sky	आकाश	aakash
712	sleep	सोना	sona
713	slowly	धीरे–धीरे	dheere-dheere

173

714	small	छोटा	chota
715	smile	मुस्कराना	muskurana
716	snake	साँप	saanp
717	snug	सुखद	sukhad
718	soldier	सैनिक	sainik
719	solid	ठोस	thos
720	some	कुछ	kuch
721	son	बेटा	beta
722	soon	जल्दी	jaldee
723	sorry	दुःखी	dukhee
724	soup	शोरबा	sorba
725	South	दक्षिण	dakshin
726	souvenir	निशानी	nishanee
727	space	अन्तरिक्ष	antariksh
728	spark	चिंगारी	chingaree

174

729	speak	बोलना	bolna
730	Special	विशेष	vises
731	speed	रफ्तार	raftar
732	spend	खर्च	kharch
733	spider	मकड़ी	makri
734	Spinach	पालक	palak
735	spot	चिती	chitee
736	square	वर्ग	warg
737	star	तारा	tara
738	station	स्थान	asthan
739	stay	ठहरना	thaharna
740	stone	पत्थर	pathar
741	stop	रोकना	rokna
742	store	भण्डार	bhandar
743	story	कहानी	kahanee

175

744	street	गली	galee
745	student	छात्र	chatra
746	study	पढ़ना	parna
747	subway	तलमार्ग	talmarg
748	such	ऐसा	aisa
749	Sugar	शक्कर	sakkar
750	Summer	ग्रीष्म	grism
751	sun	सूर्य	surya
752	Sunday	रविवार	ravivar
753	surface	पृष्ठ	pristh
754	sweep	झाड़ू देना	jharoo dena
755	sweet	मिठाई	meethee
756	swim	तैरना	tairna
757	table	मेज	mez
758	tail	पूँछ	poonch

759	tailor	दरजी	darji
760	take	लेना	lena
761	tank	टैंक	tank
762	taste	स्वाद	sawad
763	tea	चाय	chaya
764	teach	सिखाना	sikhana
765	teacher	शिक्षक	sikshak
766	teeth	दाँत	dant
767	temple	मंदिर	mandir
768	ten	दस	dus
769	thank you	धन्यवाद	dhanyawad
770	that	यह	yah
771	thaw	पिघलना	pighalna
772	theme	विषय	visay
773	then	तब	tab

774	theory	सिद्धान्त	sidhant
775	thigh	जांघ	jangh
776	think	सोचना	sochna
777	third	तीसरा	teesara
778	thirst	प्यास	payas
779	this	यह	yah
780	thorn	काँटा	kanta
781	though	यद्यपि	yadyapi
782	thousand	हजार	hazar
783	thread	धागा	dhaga
784	threat	धमकी	dhamkee
785	three	तीन	teen
786	throw	फेंकना	phekana
787	thrust	धकेलना	dhakelana
788	Thursday	गुरुवार	guruwar

789	thus	ऐसा	asisa
790	ticket	टिकट	ticket
791	tight	चुस्त	chust
792	time	समय	samay
793	tip	अग्र	agra
794	tired	थका हुआ	thak hua
795	title	शीर्षक	sirsak
796	today	आज	aaj
797	tomato	टमाटर	tamatar
798	tonic	बलवर्द्धक	balwardhak
799	too	अधिक	adhik
800	topic	विषय	visay
801	torrid	बहुत गरम	bahut garam
802	total	कुल	kul
803	tounge	जीभ	zibh

804	toy	खिलौना	khilauna
805	tragedy	त्रासदी	trasdee
806	translate	अनुवाद-	anuwad
807	trapes	घुमना-फिरना	ghuman-phirna
808	travel	यात्रा	yaatra
809	treason	देशद्रोह	deshdroh
810	tree	पेड़	perh
811	truth	सत्यता	satyata
812	try	कोशिश	kosis
813	Tuesday	मंगलवार	mangalwar
814	turmeric	हल्दी	haldee
815	twelve	बारह	barah
816	twenty	बीस	bees
817	twice	दो बार	do bar
818	twitter	चहकना	chahakna

819	two	दो	do
820	uncle	चाचा	chacha
821	understand	समझना	samajhna
822	unfaithful	बेईमान	baeman
823	university	विश्वविद्यालय	viswavidyalaya
824	unmanly	नामर्द	namard
825	unrest	असन्तोष	asantosh
826	unsafe	असुरक्षित	asurakshit
827	useful	उपयोगी	upyogee
828	vacant	खाली	khalee
829	vacation	अवकाश	avkash
830	vagrant	आवारा	aawara
831	value	मूल्य	mulya
832	vegetable	सब्जी	sabjee
833	vegetarian	शाकाहारी	Sakaharee

834	verge	सिरा	sira
835	very	बहुत	bahut
836	vexed	विवादा–स्पद	vivadaspad
837	victim	शिकार	sikar
838	village	गाँव	ganw
839	vim	उत्साह	utsah
840	visit	मिलना	milna
841	vocabulary	शब्दावली	sabdawalee
842	wait	रुकना	rukna
843	wake	जागना	jagna
844	walk	टहलना	tahalna
845	wall	दिवार	diwar
846	wash	धोना	dhona
847	waste	बरबाद	barbad
848	watch	घड़ी	gharee

849	water	पानी	paanee
850	Wednesday	बुधवार	budhwar
851	weep	रोना	rona
852	well	कुशल	kushal
853	wheat	गेहूँ	gehun
854	white	सफेद	safaid
855	who	कौन	kaun
856	whose	किसका	kiska
857	wife	पत्नी	patnee
858	wind	हवा	hawa
859	window	खिड़की	khirkee
860	wine	शराब	sarab
861	wink	झपकाना	jhapkana
862	winter	शीतकाल	seetkal
863	Wish	कामना	kamna

864	With	के साथ	ke saath
865	woman	औरत	aurat
866	wood	लकड़ी	ladkee
867	wool	ऊन	oon
868	word	शब्द	sabad
869	work	काम	kaam
870	worker	श्रमिक	shramik
871	world	संसार	sansar
872	worry	चिन्ता	chinta
873	wrath	रोष	rosh
874	write	लिखना	likhna
875	yah	वाह	wah
876	year	वर्ष	warsh
877	yellow	पीला	peela
878	yes	हाँ	han

879	yesterday	कल	kal
880	yet	अब तक	ab tak
881	yew	सदाबहार	sadabahar
882	yield	उत्पन्न करना	utpan karna
883	yielding	झुकने वाला	jhukne wala
884	yoke	जुआ	juwa
885	yore	प्राचीन काल	pracheen kaal
886	you	तुम	tum
887	young	जवान	jawan
888	your	तुम्हारा	tumhara
889	yourself	आप स्वयं	aap swayam
890	youth	किशोरावस्था	kishorawastha
891	yule	बड़ा दिन	bara din
892	zealous	उत्साही	utsahee
893	zebra	जेब्रा	zebra

894	zest	सुस्वाद	*suswad*
895	Zeus	देवराज	*devraj*
896	zigzag	टेढ़ा-मेढ़ा	*teda-meda*
897	zonate	धारीदार	*dhareedar*
898	zone	छेत्र	*kshetra*
899	zoo	चिड़ियाघर	*chidiyaghar*
900	zoom	अचानक बढ़ना	*achanak badna*

Titles in this series:

Titles in this series:

NOTES:

NOTES:

NOTES:

NOTES: